MESMERISM AND THE AMERICAN CURE OF SOULS

Mesmerism
and the
American Cure of Souls

Robert C. Fuller

UNIVERSITY OF PENNSYLVANIA PRESS
Philadelphia
1982

BF
1125
.F84
1982

Library of Congress Cataloging in Publication Data

Fuller, Robert C.
Mesmerism and the American cure of souls.

Bibliography: p.
Includes index
1. Mesmerism—United States—History—19th century.
2. United States—Religious life and customs.
I. Title.
BF1125.F84   1982   154.7'2   82-8327
ISBN 0-8122-7847-X   AACR2

Printed in the United States of America

TO KATHY

Contents

Foreword

Historians have long been fascinated with the many "isms" that surfaced and attracted followings during the nineteenth century. Transcendentalism, communitarianism, spiritualism, Adventism, and others, have been repeatedly studied and placed within the broader context of our national experience. The academic world no longer regards these movements as historical quirks. They are now viewed as legitimate indicators of important cultural processes. Each expressed popular dissatisfactions while, simultaneously, creating a vehicle for both personal and social innovations. Although mesmerism is commonly cited as somehow figuring into the period's creative self-interpretation, it has never received systematic attention. Neither a sect, experimental social program, nor a distinctive theological creed, mesmerism has managed to elude the interpretive categories of American historiography.

History is, however, as fluid as the present. Those who have been puzzled by the recent popularity of the so-called new religions realize that many cultural phenomena defy reduction to any one extant set of labels, categories, or compartmentalized vocabularies. This would be particularly true in the attempt to account for why so many of our modern psychotherapies like EST, Scientology, Jungian study groups, or Transcendental Meditation, have been able to engender genuinely religious enthusiasm in their followers. That these groups have so successfully attracted cultlike followings would seem to suggest that they have in some way built upon an array of cultural forms which, at least latently, are capable of imbuing psychological ideas with an aura of ultimacy. It is in this respect that the phenomenon of mesmerism, the nation's first popular psychology, now looms as a much larger determinant of the nineteenth-century's legacy to modern self-understanding than we had formerly observed.

That a novel European healing science would find such a receptive audience in nineteenth-century America is itself not surprising. Before 1876, when Pasteur and Koch finally isolated the role of microorganisms in producing disease, there had been a great deal of confusion as to the means of arriving at a competent diagnosis, let alone effecting a cure. Whether out of philanthropic naiveté or pecuniary self-interest, "doctors of the people" capitalized on the pervasive physical suffering of their peers. A much abused and fad-weary public learned to regard medical science with a cynicism mitigated only by its desperate desire for a more reliable program of cure.

The deplorable status of nineteenth-century medical practice explains why Americans' interests were initially aroused by mesmerism's alleged healing properties. Yet mesmerism's medical promise itself offers few hints concerning why its psychological theories subsequently developed into a full-blown philosophy of human nature. The story of mesmerism is thus very much the story of why

Americans first turned to psychological ideas in their individual quests for wholeness. The sixty-five-year period during which the nation's first psychological system emerged was a hinge period in American life. Between 1835 and 1900, rapid industrialization, urbanization, and unprecedented autonomy in intellectual pursuits combined to set the American psyche adrift from its traditional moorings. Life no longer revolved around the Puritan-inspired world view that had formerly lent meaning and direction to the American experience. The country's first major dose of secularism began to take its toll on American self-reliance, leaving many not knowing quite where to turn for assistance.

As Max Weber has so brilliantly demonstrated, popular demand for more comprehensive systems of care and guidance is a key determinant of the philosophical and theological categories which will gain ascendancy in any given era.[1] In the degree to which the troubles besetting nineteenth-century Americans were insufficiently addressed by either current medical science or regnant religious doctrines, they were destined to find their first expression through a vehicle such as mesmerism, whose intellectual contours were flexible enough to accommodate to the mental and emotional exigencies arising within popular culture. Mesmerism would, in fact, appear to be an almost paradigmatic instance of the role that popular psychologies have played in giving tangible expression to the religious yearnings of the American people.

To label the cultural functions performed by a movement such as mesmerism *religious* is, of course, to employ a very particular conception of the term *religion*. While mesmerist psychology obviously lacked the institutional structures ordinarily associated with religious commitment, it nonetheless provided the general public with a "means of ultimate transformation." That is, both in its doctrines (belief) and therapeutic practices (ritual), mesmerism framed symbolic processes through which individuals might learn to participate in some ultimate reality. As distinct from nonreligious cultural forms, mesmerism was designed to accomplish what Frederick Streng describes as the distinctively religious task of mediating a transcendent "power and insight to distinguish what is real or true from what is secondary, derivative, or even false . . . [and thereby open] new horizons for self-realization."[2] Mesmerism was thus the first psychological system to provide individuals with curative services that have traditionally been classified under the rubric *cure of souls.*[3] Its healing methods were explicitly intended to lead an individual beyond his or her own private resources to some health-bestowing power which "represents to him, however vaguely, the resources, wisdom, and authority of religion."[4] When cast in this light, a historical analysis of mesmerism would appear to mount an impressive argument that the early development of social scientific thinking in this country registered, not so much the abandonment of religious interest, but rather its divorce from apparently outmoded ecclesiastical and scriptural forms.

The course which mesmerism eventually followed during its tenure in American intellectual thought sheds historical perspective upon the ways in which popular psychologies structure their adherents' religious and ethical commitments.[5] It seems that, with the passage of time, mesmerism's theories concerning psychological regeneration proved themselves an insufficient basis for a well-rounded interpretation of human fulfillment. Mesmerist psychology was eventually forgotten altogether for the principal reason that its theories failed to help individuals learn to care responsibly for one another. In fact, mesmerism's only surviving contribution to American culture, the cult of positive thinking, continues to this day to equate psychological health with the kind of unmitigated self-seeking that characterizes the narcissistic bent of modern society.

Our historical analysis will, I believe, prove mesmerism to constitute a rich and hitherto unexplored chapter in the unchurched spirituality of the American people—a chapter which, while in many ways long-forgotten, is not for that reason without fascination for the modern reader.

Acknowledgments

Debts incurred in the academic world are rarely repaid in full; our formal acknowledgments are a feeble way of crediting the many people to whom we have repeatedly turned for advice or assistance. In my case, three former mentors have given generously of themselves by reading and commenting upon drafts of my manuscript. Jerald Brauer, Don Browning, and Martin Marty—all of the University of Chicago—made substantive contributions to this project. Don Browning gave helpful advice concerning the value of this study for placing the development of American psychology in cultural perspective. Martin Marty offered numerous hints as to how my work might lend a kind of "plausibility structure" to a style of American spirituality which has all too often been slighted by religious historians. And I will be forever grateful to Jerald Brauer, whose historiographical skills time and again helped me to locate this rather offbeat subject within the warp and woof of American Protestant culture.

Every scholar depends upon the talents of his or her colleagues. My good friend Peter Dusenbury gave pointed editorial suggestions which saved this book from being overly burdened with a variety of structural flaws. I also wish to thank my Dean, Max Kele, and Academic Vice President, John Hitt, for their earnest support of scholarly activity here at Bradley University. Additionally, both Janet Greenwood and Malcolm Call of the University of Pennsylvania Press are to be commended for their expert work in connection with the editing of this book.

My final word of thanks is reserved for my wife, Kathy, to whom this book is dedicated. Far from a passive helpmate, she takes an active interest in my work that helps animate even the most burdensome of tasks.

Chapter 1

Discovery Across the Atlantic

There is only one illness and one healing.
—*Franz Anton Mesmer, 1779*

Mesmerism, was, of course, not indigenous to the United States. The European origins of this healing science constitute a story all their own. However, this story only partially anticipates its American saga, for by the time the science of animal magnetism made passage across the Atlantic, it had evolved into a healing philosophy eminently adapted to what, it seems, were peculiarly American disorders.

Franz Anton Mesmer thrust himself upon European intellectual circles as the bearer of an epoch-making discovery.[1] The Viennese physician claimed to have successfully treated a woman suffering from a hysterical condition that afflicted her with no less than fifteen symptoms. It had been Mesmer's good fortune to observe a certain periodicity to her attacks. He astutely reasoned that, if he could find a means of artificially inducing these tidal-like fluctuations in her physical system, he might thereby be enabled to bring them under control. Mesmer instructed his patient to swallow a solution containing traces of iron and then proceeded to attach magnets to her legs and stomach. Almost instantly she began to report waves of energy flowing up and down her body. As these agitations continued to intensify, she promptly fell prey to a violent recurrence of her hysterical symptoms. After several such sessions, the frequency and severity of these magnetically controlled "crises" gradually diminished to the point where they at last disappeared altogether. The woman was pronounced permanently cured. Similar successes with other patients followed one after another until Mesmer's fame began to spread across the Continent.

Mesmer's discovery that human ailments could be explained and treated according to the presence of dynamic forces previously undetected by medical science stimulated successive theoretical breakthroughs which eventually gave rise to modern psychiatry. But to Mesmer's way of thinking, his patients' recoveries had nothing whatsoever to do with what we, today, would call psychological factors. Nor, for that matter, did he attribute his cures to the magnets per se. Rather, the curative agent was said to be an invisible energy, or fluid, which he called animal magnetism. He believed that he had at last come upon the etheric medium through which sensations of every kind—light, heat, magnetism, electricity—were able to pass from one physical object to another. Mesmer thus proclaimed animal magnetism to be a universal substance linking together every orderly process throughout nature. Moreover, this cosmic essence was also said to be more or less evenly distributed throughout the healthy human body. If for any reason an individual's supply of animal magnetism were to be thrown out of equilibrium, one or more bodily organs would consequently be deprived of sufficient amounts of this vital force and would begin to falter. Since there was only one cause of illness, it followed that there was only one truly effective mode of healing—the restoration of equilibrium to the body's supply of animal magnetism. Simply put, Mesmer believed he had reduced medical science to the passing of magnets over the patients' heads in an effort to supercharge their nervous systems with this mysterious, yet life-giving, energy.

The impact of Mesmer's discovery upon European intellectual life can only be understood with reference to the ideological struggles of the period. In the mid-eighteenth century Englightenment rationality was on the ascent. While the church still held a firm grip upon the middle and lower classes, the aristocracy was actively struggling for political and intellectual autonomy. Mesmer's healing practices brought this ideological controversy to a head. It was, in fact, his personal and professional victory over a Swiss country priest by the name of Johann Gassner which first gained him notoriety. Gassner had already received general acclaim for his exceptional practice of the magicoreligious art of exorcism. A popularly revered healing method in the European cure of souls tradition, exorcism enjoyed the theological and ecclesiastical backing of the Catholic church. Thus Gassner's cures, in both their setting and their rationale, drew upon the authority of religion to mediate between men and the suprahuman powers engulfing them.

In 1775 when Mesmer appeared before the German medical academy to demonstrate his healing powers, he proclaimed himself to be inaugurating a momentous revo-

3

lution in both the science and philosophy of his day. To all appearances Mesmer's methods were identical to Gassner's. Like Gassner he elicited pronounced attacks of his patients' diabolical symptoms with the mere touch of a finger. He, too, could make their peculiar afflictions recede and permanently disappear with simple manual gestures. But the difference, and a crucial one in his time, was that Mesmer denied that there was anything supernatural about his cures. He claimed to have discovered the scientific principle of disease of which all healers before him had been but dimly aware. His victory over Gassner was at once that of the Englightenment over the Baroque, the aristocracy over the clergy, and science over theology.[2]

A short time later Mesmer published his famous *Reflections on the Discovery of Animal Magnetism* (1779) in which he enumerated twenty-seven principles believed to form the basis of his healing science.[3] A quick glance at the more important of these reveals how thoroughly Mesmer ensconsed his theory of animal magnetism in Enlightenment rationality:

1. There exists a mutual influence between celestial bodies, the earth, and animated bodies.
2. The means of this influence is a fluid which is universally widespread and pervasive in a manner which allows for no void, subtly permits no comparison, and is of a nature which is susceptible to receive, propagate, and communicate all impressions of movement.
3. This reciprocal action is subject to mechanical laws, unknown until now.
4. This action results in alternative effects which can be considered as ebb and flow.
. . . .
6. It is by this operation (the most universal of those

4

laws which nature offers us) that active relations are exerted between the heavenly bodies, the earth, and its constituent parts.

. . . .

9. This mutual influence exhibits, particularly in the human body, properties analogous to those of a magnet. One can distinguish diverse and opposing poles which can be communicated, changed, diminished, and reinforced; even the phenomenon of declination is observed.

10. The property of an animal body which renders it susceptible to this influence of celestial bodies and of the reciprocal action of its environment evinces an analogy with a magnet so I have decided to call it "Animal Magnetism."

. . . .

22. It should be understood that magnetism and artificial electricity, with respect to illness, have qualities which are shared in common with many other agents which nature offers us; and if the administration of one of these other agents results in useful effects it is really due to animal magnetism.

23. One will notice by the facts, according to the practical rules which I establish, that this principle can immediately cure illness of the nerves and mediately all others.

Thus, in one panacean stroke, Mesmer's theory brushed both medical science and religious supernaturalism to the side. The doctrine of animal magnetism reduced nature's established means of regulating physical and human affairs to a simple formula. Mesmer had laid hold of a principle that deflated the pretensions of rival healing systems by subsuming them under one grand doctrine. "There is," he pontificated, "only one illness and one healing." The obvious implication was that conventional medicine was largely useless; any therapeutic value attributed to either religious or medical healing practices was owing only to their indirect effect upon the patient's supply of animal magnetism. Mesmer's methods were more direct. With sufficient concentration and willpower, a healer could capacitate, store, and transmit potent energies from his own person to the patient. The science of animal magnetism was alone sufficient to "immediately cure illness of the nerves and mediately all others."

Word of Mesmer's "discovery" spread rapidly across the Continent, prompting him to leave Vienna for Paris where he was received as a celebrity. There Mesmer's reputation soared ever higher as a wealthy aristocracy fled to his doorstep in hopes of witnessing, if not actually becoming participants in, his medical revolution. His more affluent disciples paid large sums of money for the privilege of membership in the newly formed Society of Harmony. The Society instructed loyal pupils in its well-kept secrets pertaining to the technical application of Mesmer's theories. Members were required to swear an oath of fealty to both the Society and Mesmer himself before the intricacies of wielding animal magnetic influence could be divulged to them. Once chartered by the Society of Harmony, they were permitted to open practices of their own.

If during all of this Mesmer's ego waxed grandiose, the methods of his cure became even more so. He soon abandoned the use of magnets in favor of the much celebrated *baquet*. This strange device amounted to little more than a large oaken tub around which up to twenty people at a single sitting could be supercharged with animal magnetism. Inside the tub were placed iron rods connecting patients to specially "magnetized" jars of water. Mesmer would don a lilac-colored cape, play on his glass harmonica for the ostensible purpose of generating additional sanative vibrations, and prance about waving a wand at one patient after another. His patients graciously responded by falling into pronounced "crises" and emerged from this dramatic affair claiming cure.

All of this did not go unnoticed by the well-entrenched medical establishment, which, with not a little jealousy, finally demanded a thorough investigation. Two separate governmental commissions were formed to examine Mesmer's practices. Participation by the most-distinguished scientists of the day, including Bailly; Lavoisier; and the American statesman-inventor, Benjamin Franklin (who, incidentally, never took an active part in the proceedings), attests to the degree of controversy which Mesmer had aroused at the highest levels of French society.

The commissions' final reports included a synopsis of the medical records of over one hundred patients who were currently undergoing treatment at the hands of one of Mesmer's most reputable pupils.[4] All but six had already evidenced marked progress; over one-half claimed complete cure. The ailments included spleen infections, rheumatism, asthma, headaches, skin diseases, as well as various nervous disorders. These documents make it difficult to escape the conclusion that hundreds of persons who had proved incurable by conventional medical practices had found substantial, if not permanent, cure at the hands of Mesmer and his colleagues. Just how to interpret these cures was and still is another matter.

From the outset the commissions proceeded under the assumption that cures alone were of ephemeral scientific importance. The substantive issue at stake was the alleged existence of a new physical substance called animal magnetism. This was a proposition which admitted of rigorous scientific investigation. Commissioners monitored several healing treatments, using the newest scientific instruments available to them. Alas, no palpable evidence could be found to indicate the transmission of any electrical or magnetic force. Their reports concluded that "there is no proof of the existence of Animal Magnetism; that this fluid, having no existence, has in consequence no utility."[5] And as for the undeniable curative value of Mesmer's practices? It was promptly dismissed as the mere product of the patients' own "imaginations."

Many of the patients protested that the commissioners' reports did disservice to the actual facts. They claimed to have had vivid awareness of animal magnetism entering their bodies. Some professed to have felt alternating hot and cold currents; others saw emanations of the fluid streaming from the operator's hands. All of this had been deemed by the investigative panels as without serious scientific value. Such phenomena were obviously the products of overactive imaginations. Unfortunately, no one paused to ponder just what a wondrous faculty the mesmerists had demonstrated the imagination to be.

The commissions' reports signaled the beginning of the end of Mesmer's Parisian tenure. His fall from aristocratic grace was further accelerated by his personal arrogance. Highly egocentric and possessing a volatile temper, Mesmer managed to offend nearly everyone upon whom he might have relied for loyalty and support. Within a short period of time, he and his peculiar practices had become thoroughly discredited and made an object of popular satire. The press lampooned mesmerists as just so many charlatans bilking a gullible public. Mesmer was finally forced to retreat to a country cottage near Lake Constance, where he lived in seclusion until his death in 1815.

However, despite the findings of the two commissions, Mesmer's theories continued to attract a coterie of enthusiastic advocates. For a brief period mesmerism even reigned as the queen of European sciences. Historian Robert Darnton argues that the favorable reception mesmerism continued to receive reflects the "popular mind" of late eighteenth-century Europe. He reminds us that mesmerism offered the Frenchman of the 1780s "a serious explanation of Nature, of her wonderful, invisible forces, and even in some cases of the forces governing society and politics."[6]

Mesmer's theories appeared congenial to the various utopian sentiments then afoot on the Continent. Many prerevolutionary Frenchmen were eager for ideas that could pierce beneath the artifice of an encrusted social order and uncover the wellsprings of universality and brotherhood. The discovery that nature's forces could be harnessed and used to restore harmony to physical systems reinforced even the most idealistic of aspirations. For many the doctrine of animal magnetism proved that physical health, moral improvement, and social progress could all be lawfully engineered. Ever more utopian interpretations of Mesmer's discovery were offered until it became inextricably bound up with radical politics on the one hand and various forms of mysticism on the other. Darnton finds that the successive developments in the popular understanding of mesmerism provide "guidelines to the subtle transformations of popular attitudes during the periods generally labeled as the age of Reason and the age

9

of Romanticism."[7] The reason for mesmerism's pivotal position in this fundamental reorientation of Europeans' world views is not difficult to ascertain; quite by accident the mesmerists uncovered a depth to human experience which defied reduction into the mechanistic categories of Enlightenment (and Mesmer's own) rationality and, for that reason, appeared to lend plausibility to whatever ideological currents were underfoot.

It was Mesmer's most capable disciple, the Marquis de Puységur, who actually brought lasting significance to the science of animal magnetism. With Puységur magnetic healing took a wholly new direction, one leading straight to the subconscious mind. Ironically, by the time his healing science reached the United States, the term *mesmerism* actually referred to Puységur's rather than to Mesmer's discoveries.

Puységur magnetized his patients only to have them fall into unusual, sleeplike states of consciousness: They were, so to speak, "mesmerized." Entranced persons were much more interesting than they ever were under normal circumstances. Most appeared far brighter and much more perceptive of the subtle nuances in interpersonal relationships. And more important, whenever they were consulted as to the nature of someone's illness, they promptly offered a complete case history and diagnosis which invariably held up under subsequent investigation. Many even prescribed remedies and forecasted timetables for the eventual course of recovery. A select few of Puységur's subjects attained an even deeper state of consciousness, which he described as one of "extraordinary lucity." These subjects spontaneously performed feats of telepathy, clairvoyance, and precognition. Puységur found him-

somnambulic state as an anesthetic during surgical operations.[9] Their work gave yet further demonstration to the reality and potential utility of a distinct realm of consciousness seemingly independent of the ordinary waking state.

While the story is far too long for us to review here, mesmerism gradually, almost imperceptibly, merged into the burgeoning field of dynamic psychiatry.[10] Jean-Martin Charcot, Pierre Janet, and yet another young Viennese iconoclast, Sigmund Freud, wove the data furnished by entranced patients into psychoanalytic orthodoxy. Now referred to as hypnosis, the act of inducting persons into an entranced state of consciousness had finally received the backing of the scientific and medical communities. However, the later champions of hypnosis were so eager to gain scientific respectability for the fledgling field of psychiatry that they either ignored or vehemently repudiated many of the supranormal phenomena long associated with the trance state. They were quick to accredit the trance state as the royal road to a unique stratum of consciousness. They also insisted that their patients, when brought into contact with their unconscious selves, were instantly afforded greater self-understanding and emotional well-being. Some even admitted that their patients thereby became so perceptive to interpersonal communication that the rapport between patient and therapist offered positive support to the hypothesis of telepathy or direct thought transference.[11] But with the possible exception of Carl Jung, the psychoanalytic school restricted any normative considerations of mental life to the domain of ego operations. Feats such as clairvoyance or the willful emanation of nonmaterial energies were, thus, theoretically impossible. Psychoanalysis distanced itself from its cloudy origins by sharply denouncing the mesmerists' claims as the product of a new psychiatric catchall, "suggestibility."

European mesmerists found themselves increasingly relegated to the outer fringes of scientific respectability. They made every effort to defend themselves by attempting to reconcile their "fluidic" explanations of the mesmeric state with other, more properly psychological, ones. Puységur led the way in forging a middle ground between Mesmer's twenty-seven principles and the newly emerging scientific psychiatry. He was among the first to state that it was possible to transmit animal magnetism without physical apparatus such as magnets or the *baquet*. Puységur also conceded that a patient's suggestibility, will, and prior expectations were important variables affecting his susceptibility to the operator's influence. But mesmerism, even in its more interpersonal and psychological versions, never abandoned the doctrine of an invisible fluid. Physical cure and paranormal mental activities were alike irreducible to a self-contained ego. Mesmerism distinguished itself from opposing theories by its continued commitment to the existence of some mysterious substance capable of linking human consciousness to some transpersonal psychic reality.

New theories were constantly advanced. One French mesmerist, Deleuze, argued that animal magnetism was the soul's modus operandi for influencing the body. His subjects described animal magnetism as a thin, fluidic atmosphere enveloping the human body. Although this fluid was in some respects analogous to the nerve-force of the body, Deleuze identified it as a spiritual substance quite independent of material reality. He explained that under the peculiar condition of the mesmeric state, the mind becomes so attuned to this universal medium of sensation that ideas and objects enter directly into our thoughts without the mediation of the physical senses.

Mesmer, too, eventually revised his theories so as to take clairvoyance and telepathy more fully into account. He concluded that animal magnetism is transmitted from operator to patient through an "inner sense." Dormant in the normal waking state of consciousness, this inner sense is responsible for the mental functions occurring spontaneously to subjects under the influence of the magnetic condition. When properly activated, this inner sense bypasses ordinary sense modalities and brings the mind into direct rapport with the principle behind sensations of every kind—animal magnetism. Perhaps this was the "imagination" which had effected his magnetic cures.

When all was said and done, the European fascination with mesmerism never really moved beyond the level of parlor-room frivolity. Mesmerism became just one more passing fad that entertained an idle upper class.

For a short time German romanticists believed that mesmerism offered palpable evidence for their notion of an omnipresent World Soul. But outside of sporadic outcroppings of interest among Swedenborgians, Rosicrucians, and various theosophical groups, it failed it have a long-lasting impact on European philosophical or religious thought.[12] European intellectuals still subscribed to the basic tenents of their time-honored institutions. Political, medical, and religious spheres of life were well differentiated and neatly compartmentalized. Mesmerism never produced the proper credentials to achieve enduring status within any of the three. Nor was it able to secure for itself a cultural niche by totally blurring the distinctions between them as it was later to do in America. Apparently

Europe lacked a crisis for which animal magnetism was an appropriate cure.

By contrast, mesmerism found America still without institutions cohesive enough to impart order to personal and social life. In a directionless but ever-expanding social environment, Americans were in sore need of doctrines that would ease the burden of systematic inner-direction. In the period between 1800 and 1850 Americans evidenced what could only be described as a congenital susceptibility to a wide assortment of religious sects and utopian social movements. Each competed for converts by promulgating simplistic moral and intellectual doctrines especially adapted to the exigencies of frontier life. As we shall see, mesmerism's early development in the United States owed a great deal to its apparent affinity with these enthusiastic sects.

Mesmerism's subsequent progress in the United States was intimately bound up with the life of popular culture. We must remember that it entered into American intellectual life prior to the establishment of an independent psychological science. Psychology was still considered to be a minor adjunct to both philosophy and theological homiletics. Nor were there as yet any academic departments attempting to accumulate psychological knowledge through detached and systematic inquiry. Parlor-room and stage demonstrations were, thus, mesmerism's only laboratories; its theories were advanced in public lecture halls and small metaphysical clubs. Although, in Europe, mesmerism had been the privileged possession of an idle aristocracy, here it was pressed into the service of a large middle class. It should not be surprising, then, that the story of American mesmerism is also the story of shifting patterns in nineteenth-century American cultural life.

Chapter 2

The Inoculation Works Wonders

*. . . an order of phenomena so important to science and so glori-
ous to human nature.*
—*Charles Poyen, 1837*

Although mesmerism reached the zenith of its European popularity by the mid-1780s, its exportation to the United States was slow and sporadic. Of anecdotal interest is the fact that Lafayette had hoped to proselytize for the science of animal magnetism during his campaign to America. He wrote Washington in 1784 that "a German doctor named Mesmer, having made the greatest discovery about animal magnetism, has trained some pupils, among whom your humble servant is considered one of the most enthusiastic. . . . Before leaving I will obtain permission to let you into Mesmer's secret, which, you can count on it, is a great philosophical discovery."[1] The most formidable opponent Lafayette encountered in this crusade proved to be Thomas Jefferson. Appalled by the irrational excesses to which this "great philosophical discovery" had led in France, Jefferson hastened to ward off Lafayette's mes-

meric invasion by distributing copies of the negative conclusions reached by the two French commissions. Perhaps
Jefferson overreacted; for, as it turned out, Lafayette never
did receive permission to dispense Mesmer's great secret
to those in the New World. It was to be a few more years
before this magnetic fluid, ostensibly present throughout
nature, would successfully cross the Atlantic.

America's first full dose of animal magnetism came from
the tongue of a Frenchman named Charles Poyen. A self-
proclaimed Professor of Animal Magnetism, Poyen em-
barked upon a lecture tour across New England in 1836.[2]
Much to his own consternation, he found himself lecturing
upon a subject virtually unknown to his American audiences. Poyen's impassioned attempts to acquaint them
with "well authenticated facts concerning an order of phenomena so important to science and so glorious to human
nature" met considerable apathy, scorn, and derision. Or,
at least, so Poyen liked to think. Like most of the early
American mesmerists, he seemed to revel in his role as
champion of an unpopular cause. His was the mission of
a martyr, prophet, or bearer of a great truth whose time
had not quite come. Poyen likened himself to Galileo, Columbus, and Christ; he, too, had come upon a truth beyond the comprehension of the general public.

Mesmerism, he claimed, was revealing lawful principles
long hidden beneath the appearances of the outer world.
The facts to which it attested pertained to a level of reality
its detractors had never even imagined to exist. More important, the science of animal magnetism was not dealing
with neutral scientific propositions that could be accepted
or rejected with little personal consequence. Quite the
contrary. Poyen believed mesmerism to be unveiling the

17

hidden secret of human happiness and well-being. Members of the audience were called upon to make a decision, a personal commitment concerning the existence of a wider reality in which they purportedly moved and had their real being.

Poyen, like his French mentor Puységur, believed that the single most important discovery made by the science of animal magnetism was that of the somnambulic state. His public lectures consequently revolved around an actual demonstration of the magnetic state of consciousness and all of its attendant phenomena.[3] In addition to employing the services of a professional somnambule, Poyen also made a practice of enlisting a few volunteers from the audience. He explained to his subjects that his manual gestures would heighten the activity of their systems' animal magnetism to the point where what he called "external sensibilities" would temporarily recede into a sleeplike condition. Whatever the explanation, he succeeded in putting about half of his volunteers into a state of trance in which they became peculiarly unresponsive to their surroundings. Loud hand clapping and jars of ammonia passed under their noses failed to evoke even the slightest response. To all appearances, their minds had withdrawn from the physical world. These staged exhibitions proved to be great theater. Crowds thronged to see their friends and relatives transformed right before their eyes. The entertainment value of these demonstrations of the mesmeric state certainly outstripped their application to contemporary medical science. The frivolity which inevitably developed during the demonstrations had the further consequence of disenfranchising mesmerism from the established scientific community. But for all their unintended disservice to the science of animal magnetism, Poyen's lecture-demonstrations effectively stimulated the public's imagination with novel "facts" about human nature—facts which, if not as "important to science" as Poyen had hoped, would prove far more "glorious to human nature" than even he had ever dreamed.

Many of Poyen's volunteers came in hope of obtaining a medical cure. He obliged by making "passes" with his hands in an effort to direct the flow of animal magnetism to the appropriate part of the body. A large proportion of those receiving this treatment awoke from their mesmeric sleep and, remembering nothing of what had transpired, claimed cure. Poyen's own account, in many cases supported with newspaper reports and letters to the editor, lists successful treatment of such disorders as rheumatism, nervousness, back troubles, and liver ailments. He also notes that, after hearing one of his lectures, a dentist performed oral surgery upon a "twenty year old healthy male" patient to whom he gave no other anesthetic than that of rendering him into the magnetic condition.

Poyen reported that roughly 10 percent of his entranced subjects attained the "highest degree" of the magnetic condition. Their behavior went beyond the peculiar to the extraordinary. The onset of this stage in the mesmerizing process was marked by the formation of an especially intense rapport between the subject and the operator. The crucial ingredient of this rapport was the establishment of some nonverbal means of communication through which the subject could telepathically receive unspoken thoughts from the operator. Most attributed this ability to their heightened receptivity to animal magnetism. Some actually reported feeling animal magnetism impinge upon their nervous systems. They felt prickly sensations running up and down their bodies. Others claimed to "see" dazzling bright lights. Nor was it uncommon for subjects who had come into direct contact with these subtle streams of sensation to perform feats of clairvoyance and extrasensory perception spontaneously. They might locate lost objects, describe events transpiring in distant locales, or telepathically read the minds of persons in the audience. Yet, upon returning to the waking state, they remembered little of their trance-bound experiences. It was as if they had been existing in another realm altogether. They knew only that they were now more refreshed, energetic, and healed of their former ailments.

Word of Poyen's fantastic healing methods spread throughout New England. His 1837 treatise on the progress of animal magnetism in New England declares that "nineteen months have elapsed since that period and already Animal Magnetism has sprung from a complete state of obscurity and neglect into general notice, and become the object of a lively interest throughout the country."[4] Newspapers began to take notice. The *Providence Journal* reported that more than one hundred cases of "Magnetic Somnambulism" had been reported in Rhode Island alone. Poyen's system was, according to one observer, fast becoming a "steady theme of interest in New England papers" and making "a deep impression upon some of the soundest and best balanced minds."[5] Poyen cited articles from Rhode Island, Maine, and Connecticut supporting his contention that the science of animal magnetism had become a topic of conversation in all classes of society, especially—as he was quick to point out—with the learned and well-to-do.

It is not difficult to see why. Poyen was an able and evocative speaker. A former activist in the abolition movement and the author of a pamphlet detailing methods for promoting the spirit of Christianity, Poyen was merely shifting the focus of his evangelical zeal. He now played upon the growing public confidence in the ability of science to help initiate a utopian order. He prophesied that, when fully accepted by the "intelligent and fast progressing" American people, mesmerism was destined to make them "the most perfect nation on earth."[6] In this way Poyen not only helped launch mesmerism into the surging tide of American nationalism, but also assimilated it to the Jacksonian era's belief in the ultimate perfectibility of society through the progressive improvement of its individual citizens. And by appealing to deeply rooted beliefs concerning the manifest destiny of the nation, Poyen quite unwittingly hastened the identification of magnetic cures with other programs for personal rejuvenation then enjoying the enthusiastic support of various New England constituencies.

In Chapter 4 we shall take a much closer look at how mesmerism entered into the stock of ideas employed by those who wished to extend the period's progressivist temperament into the religious sphere. Here we might anticipate this discussion by alerting ourselves to the important ways in which the explanations given for the remarkable phenomena of mesmerism resembled those offered by antebellum Protestant revivalists as they, too, set about describing the lawful process of personal rejuvenation.

According to Poyen, mesmerism was to be thought of as the science of man's "moral and intellectual constitution." He insisted that its theories were not a matter of "a priori views, mere doctrines, or opinions." Mesmerism was "on the contrary, a science of observation . . . standing on the results of repeated sifted, and positive experiments."[7] A foreigner, Poyen never quite appreciated the ease with which his science of the moral constitution was to precipitate progressivist tendencies in the popular religious climate. Those wishing to test philosophical or theological doctrines by the doctrine's ability to produce the experience of inner-transformation could not help but see the far-reaching implications of mesmerism's bold claims.

Poyen had done little to transform the theory he had learned in Europe. To his way of thinking, mesmerism was a natural science and the properties of animal magnetism could all be reduced to lawful operations similar to those of other natural forces. It did not occur to him that there might be something supernatural about animal magnetism or the marvels it evoked. He simply believed phenomena such as visions of dazzling bright light or spontaneous clairvoyance to be part of the natural order that had been lawfully established according to divine will at the time of creation.

Mesmerism's earliest American enthusiasts saw these extraordinary happenings in a slightly different light. One letter addressed to the editor of the *Boston Recorder* in February 1837 reads:

George was *converted from materialism to Christianity* by the facts in Animal Magnetism developed under his [Poyen's] practice . . . *it proves the power of mind over matter* . . . *informs our faith* in the spirituality and immortality of our nature, and encourages us to *renewed efforts* to live up to its transcendent powers.[8]

A high school teacher testified that her healing was so miraculous as to convince her that "God and eternity are the only answer to these mysterious phenomena—these apparitions of the Infinity and the Unknown."[9]

Once inoculated with this foreign substance, the American popular mind evidenced immediate and well-pronounced reactions. A fairly common strain was reported by William Stone.[10] A former U.S. ambassador to the Netherlands, editor of the New York *Communal Advertiser,* and superintendent of the New York public schools, Stone's interest in mesmerism suggests that even the upper reaches of American society were susceptible to new explanations concerning the mind and its powers. The fact that he had also been an active campaigner for various moral reforms, particularly the causes of abolition and compulsory public education, would seem to make the additional point that concern with the mesmeric trance state was fully compatible with moral seriousness and earnest concern for philanthropic activity. In any case, it is a matter of record that in 1837 Stone's progressive energies were given new direction following his attendance at one of Poyen's lecture-demonstrations.

Stone was concerned that his interest in mesmerism not be regarded as that of a simpleton. He assured his readers that he, too, had at first found the tales of magical happenings occurring to entranced individuals as too incredible to be reckoned with by sober minds. It was only upon the advice of a distinguished prelate of the Episcopal church that he ever conceded to give mesmerism closer attention. Poyen's exhibitions eradicated any further doubts and made a true believer of him. Not one to sit passively at the sidelines, Stone decided to begin conducting experiments of his own. American mesmerism was moving from the public stage into the living rooms of a curious public.

Stone's investigations were typical of the many experiments conducted in private homes throughout New England in the 1830s and 40s. Like other early American mesmerists, Stone was concerned that he be regarded as a highly objective investigator. His narrative offers minutely detailed descriptions of his subjects, the experimental conditions, and the witnesses present. Since the integrity of those in attendance was the only real measure of the trustworthiness or credibility of his findings, Stone took care to convince his readers of their impeccable character. We are told that the governor of New York, several state senators, a clergyman, and three prosperous businessmen were among those who attended his experiments. Of course, none of these individuals had received formal scientific training, but their presence does show that reasonably astute persons found mesmerism worthy of their consideration.

The best known of Stone's experiments was one involving a young woman who, we are told, had been involved in an accident that had deranged her nervous system and left her blind for life. The purpose of placing her in the magnetic state was not, however, to effect a cure. Stone thought it more important to garner further evidence about the magnetic faculty of "vision without the use of visual organs." Neither Stone nor his guests were disappointed in the young woman's mesmeric abilities. She disclosed the contents of sealed envelopes, revealed the location of objects previously hidden about the room, and "read" the minds of everyone present. Since he and his

24

witnesses had taken every possible precaution against fraud, Stone confidently concluded that mesmerism was on the verge of overturning every known theory concerning the powers of the human mind.[11]

Stone carefully recorded his experiments in a letter to an interested physician. This letter was later published in pamphlet form and went through three editions in a matter of months. One of mesmerism's earliest detractors, Charles Durant, was quick to contest Stone's account.[12] Durant claimed that Stone had been the victim of a clever ruse. He offered evidence suggesting that the young woman was not blind at all. On the contrary, she saw only too clearly how she might earn herself some notoriety and, for that matter, easy money. Durant believed that, in the course of their long interview with the "entranced" subject, Stone and his colleagues had unwittingly supplied her with all the information she needed to pull off her sham. The only mystery about mesmerism was the gullibility of its adherents.

Upon reading of the controversy, Poyen felt obliged to join the fray by issuing a public rejoinder of his own.[13] He charged that Durant himself was out to make a few dollars at the expense of the public's welfare. Durant, he argued, never understood the science of animal magnetism in the first place. His diatribe against it therefore amounted to little more than the musings of an "ignorant scribbler."[14] Poyen credited Stone with having performed a great service in bringing this "science of the psychological constitution of man" to the attention of New England. He went on, however, to chide Stone for having merely satisfied his own curiosity about the clairvoyant faculty; any well-read man should already have acknowledged it as a regularly occurring feature of the ecstatic state. It would have been far better to pursue philosophical explanations for these phenomena. For example, repeated investigations of mesmerized subjects had proved that nearly 80 percent obey the operator's unspoken commands (e.g., to stand up and move from one seat to another); yet no one had advanced a convincing explanation of how mesmerism was able to make nonphysical communication possible. Poyen himself was unsure but tentatively proposed that "[while] I know this will appear ridiculous . . . every human being carries within himself a nervous, magnetic or vital atmosphere."[15] Putting another person into a magnetic trance somehow entailed making him acutely receptive to one's own mental emanations. What Poyen found so disconcerting about Stone's experiments was that they never attempted to advance this or any other explanation for the observed phenomena. To put it another way, Poyen was disgruntled that Stone could so readily skip past mesmerism's contributions to science in his rush to display glorious, new dimensions of human nature.

Poyen returned to France in 1839. This same year an Englishman by the name of Robert Collyer began a lecture tour in America which was to carry mesmerism's sensational discoveries all along the Atlantic seaboard. The diary he kept and later published under the title *Lights and Shadows of American Life* does for early American psychology what de Tocqueville did for American democracy.[16] From the perspective of an outsider, he offers succinct observations of the period's cultural landscape to help explain why particular conceptions of human nature were able to gain such a strong foothold.

A student of Spurzheim and author of his own *Manual*

of Phrenology, Collyer had come to America with the intention of enlightening its citizens about the virtues of the science of phrenology.[17] Upon his arrival Collyer found American culture to be far more chaotic than he had anticipated. Its institutions lacked authority. Government and business were corrupt. The legal and economic spheres were wholly without consistent principles of conduct. Nowhere could he find the well-ordered society he had known in Europe. He was unable to locate a proper cultural place for anything, much less put it there. Fortunately he believed himself in possession of a philosophical system perfectly suited to redress these national deficiencies. For if phrenology could do nothing else, it could at least arrange human existence into clearly defined and differentiated compartments.

The areas most in need of tidying up were religion and medicine. Collyer was utterly dumbfounded by the street-corner evangelism of rival religious sects. He disdainfully commented that "any unlettered biped who has sufficient cant and hypocrisy may become a minister of the Gospels." Medical physicians were equally bereft of integrity. Collyer found a sufficient number of them all right but soon discovered that "half of them cannot read nor write their name." "America," he observed, "is a place where any one who has the impudence may leave the lapstone and become a physician."[18] American medicine was a grab bag of idiosyncratic remedies ranging from crude surgical techniques to sundry bottled tonics. Bedecking every street corner were handbills and posters, each advertising a different system of cure. "Daily some poor unfortunate falls a victim to these murderous quacks. Their deeds of darkness and iniquity fairly outherods Herod."

It was against this caricature of American culture that Collyer set forth the moral and intellectual advantages of the phrenological philosophy. Phrenologists had discovered that each and every human trait had its own physiological center in the brain. Protrusions or recesses of the skull were accurate indicators of a person's strengths and weaknesses. Collyer informed his audiences that a science of the brain could systematize both the religious and medical departments. A trained phrenologist could examine the shape of someone's head and make precise diagnoses as to which moral faculties were structurally deficient. Compensatory programs could then be designed and specifically adapted to the individual's mental and moral self-improvement.

Collyer had but briefly studied mesmerism prior to his American tour. He found its theories and methods to be natural extensions of phrenological theory and, in fact, ones which allowed for quicker, more startling transformations in an individual's character. Finding himself the nearest thing to an expert on mesmerism, Collyer began lecturing on the subject in large eastern cities, including Philadelphia, New York, and Boston. At first he found it difficult to convince Americans of the veracity of this strange-sounding medical theory. Mesmerism's non-materialistic explanation of disease was particularly ridiculed by the narrow-minded medical profession. But, Collyer tells us, mesmerism "always triumphed" in the eyes of the public. Large audiences flocked to get a first-hand look.

Three months of nightly lectures in Boston aroused the attention of "large and intelligent audiences." The city council finally deemed it necessary to appoint a committee "consisting of twenty-four gentlemen selected from the learned professions" to investigate Collyer's practices.[19] The committee refused to give mesmerism its full endorsement but did assure the citizenry that there was no "humbuggery" involved in Collyer's demonstrations. They even went on record as corroborating the major issue at stake in the public controversy: the reality of a distinct mesmeric state. The report concludes that "while this committee refrains from expressing any opinion as to the the science or principle of animal magnetism, they freely confess that in the experiments of Dr. Collyer, certain appearances have been presented which cannot be explained upon the supposition of collusion, or by reference to any physiological principle known to them."[20] Unlike its French counterpart, this committee was of and for the people. Its members were not about to discredit the doctrine of animal magnetism for the reason that it failed to make substantive contributions to physical science. The discovery of previously untapped human potentials was not to be lightly dismissed.

Collyer and Poyen had aroused sufficient interest to assure mesmerism's continued presence in the public limelight. In 1837 Thomas C. Hartshorn published an English translation of the French mesmerist Deleuze's *Practical Instructions in Animal Magnetism.* As the title implies, Deleuze's book amounted to a do-it-yourself manual for inducting individuals into the mesmeric state. Another work appeared that same year describing the philosophy of animal magnetism and the means for "manipulation adopted to produce ecstasy and somnambulism."[21] Scores of such books, often in convenient pamphlet form, rapidly appeared to meet the growing consumer interest created by itinerant mesmerists. One widely circulated pamphlet bore the fitting title *The History and Philosophy of Animal Magnetism with Practical Instructions for the Exercise of This Power.* Its author estimated that by 1843 there were between twenty and thirty mesmerists lecturing in New England and more than two hundred "magnetizers" practicing in Boston alone.[22]

In sharp contrast to mesmerism's European experience where it remained the guarded secret of a privileged aristocracy, the American strain of animal magnetism had been injected into the lives of a large middle class. This proved to be of no small consequence. Over the next few decades several otherwise average Americans used its discoveries to symbolize and heal a spiritual disquietude they shared with their contemporaries. Phineas P. Quimby, Andrew Jackson Davis, and Mary Baker Eddy were every bit as much beneficiaries as popularizers of mesmerist-based theories of human nature. Their ability to put psychological ideas into the service of spiritual needs paved the way for an entirely new mode of unchurched American religiosity.

The apparent ease of inducing mesmeric trance was, however, also responsible for mesmerism's inevitable extension into lowbrow culture. Quick to capitalize on this latest sensation, enterprising showmen drew large crowds to witness what amounted to little more than stage hypnotism. Mesmerism was for them nothing more than mass entertainment. Charlatanry and obvious collusion permeated sideshow exhibitions of the mind's mysterious powers. Entranced subjects mindlessly following out even the most-ludicrous commands given by the operator made mesmerism's findings appear frivolous.

An article written in 1849 entitled "Animal Magnetism" bemoaned this degeneration. The author observed how "the most successful mesmeric exhibitors in our country at the present time, instead of going through the magical passes which were formerly universally practiced and believed to be indispensable conditions . . . now rely merely upon assertions and commands."[23] The danger was thought to be real; these subjects might not be entering the deeper levels of the magnetic condition at all. Instead of supercharging their subjects' nervous systems with animal magnetism, operators were instead merely commanding them into a state of acquiescence. Once under the operators' verbal dominance subjects could, for example, be told

> that a handkerchief held before them is a snake: they believe it, and manifest the natural alarm and terror of the object. This class of experiments is highly amusing and gratifying to the public although it proves nothing more than the well known powers of imagination. It conveys no new scientific or philosophic instruction, and virtually tends, by demonstrating the extraordinary power of the imagination, *to conceal from our view the most important* phrenological laws and actual nervous influences of man.[24]

Stage hypnotism, while sensational in its own right, was diverting attention from mesmerism's cardinal postulate—the existence of a subtle energy capable of exerting a healing influence upon the human nervous system.

Nor was banality the only crime of which these professional magnetizers were suspected. Many citizens were ill disposed toward the idea that someone with highly developed mental powers should be allowed to gain complete control over another person's mind. Those who believed strong willpower to be the only deterrent against errant human tendencies were naturally disgusted by a theory requesting people to passively abandon themselves to another's will. As one commentator put it, magnetism was potentially "an agent of great abuse and impropriety."[25] What secret commands might be implanted into the unsuspecting subject's mind? What unknown power might an unscrupulous operator secure over a trusting volunteer? And mightn't this mysterious animal magnetic fluid be Satan's means for claiming innocent souls? An insight into the kinds of impressions mesmerism made upon educated New Englanders can be gleaned from the tirades of a New York physician. In his opinion, mesmerism could be lumped together with phrenology, ultratemperance, and ultrasectarianism as one of the many quackeries and humbugs currently subverting the social order.[26] He pointed out that the theory of animal magnetism asked people to resign their reason, imagine an absurdity, and forget common sense. In short, it took advantage of human gullibility. The itinerant mesmerists, each accompanied by a factory girl who would rather sleep than do honest work for a living, were bilking the public of their dollar admissions. Oddly enough, he stopped short of claiming that mesmerism consisted entirely of the fraudulent deceptions of clever factory girls. He evidently found mesmerism's claims sufficiently plausible to warn the public against the possibility that mesmerists might soon begin destroying human life at pleasure through the misuse of their powers.

Others saw something still far more unsettling in this mysterious philosophy. There were sexual overtones to the mesmerizing process which were too obvious to be discretely overlooked. It was, after all, an act which often required a passive female to willingly yield all mental resistance and to comply with the physical gestures of an active, dominating male. How could anyone help but suspect baser passions at work? In fact, certain members of the French commissions had secretly submitted a supplementary report to the king warning of the indecencies to which Mesmer's science was inherently prone. Deleuze even devoted an entire section of his book to precautions to be followed in selecting a magnetizer. It was best, he counseled, for women to be magnetized by other women, since subjects commonly develop a deep affection for their operator. He also warned that magnetized women often make "spasmodic movements" of a nature too improper for mixed company.

A pamphlet containing the confessions of a Boston magnetizer confirmed the public's worst suspicions.[27] His past experiences as a mesmeric operator convinced him that these strange practices generated a power that was, without question, an effective agent in healing both physical and nervous disorders. Moreover, he, too, believed that the magnetic condition established a telepathic bond between the subject and the operator. But a contrite conscience prompted him to forewarn the public against this "hydraheaded agency" and the improprieties to which it all too easily led. He confessed to have surrendered, quite against his original intentions, to fleeting temptations and to have telepathically impressed affections for himself upon the minds of lovely young ladies. Time after time he had been unable to resist the seductive appeal of beautiful women utterly subjecting themselves to him while grasp-

33

ing his hand and gazing trustingly into his eyes. By skill-fully employing his mesmeric powers, he had succeeded in stirring their passions toward him to such a degree that they became willing to commit indecencies. Mesmerism, he implied, was an agent eminently capable of subverting moral sensibilities.

Public indignation at these improprieties in the use of mesmeric powers had long-lasting consequences upon general attitudes toward mesmerism and its new discov-ery, the subconscious mind. Alongside those who viewed mesmerism as a royal road to spiritual utopia were those who feared the power of one individual to gain unre-stricted control over the innermost thoughts of another. The period's literature registers the differing images which the doctrine of animal magnetism conjured up in the minds of nineteenth-century Americans. For instance, Emerson recognized that mesmerism offered a clue to the unfathomable mysteries of life. Its phenomena, he con-cluded, "belong to the copious chapter of Demonology under which category I suppose everybody's experience might have a chapter."[28] The champion of a philosophy of self-reliance, Emerson shuddered at the thought that "an adept should attempt to put me asleep by the concen-tration of his will without my leave."[29] His counsel con-cerning the science of animal magnetism? "Keep away from keyholes."

Nathaniel Hawthorne's assessment was more complex. He was at first intrigued by the mysteries surrounding the mesmeric state. Hawthorne shared the popular opinion that mesmerism could be used to discover and systematize knowledge unattainable through rational investigation. A diary entry from 1842 records his own list of "questions as to unsettled points of History and Mysteries of Nature to be asked of mesmerized persons."[30] But when mesmerism enters into the plot of *The House of the Seven Gables,* it is for the more mundane query of ascertaining the whereabouts of a lost document. The attempt is unsuccessful, but Hawthorne's mesmerist finds other uses for his superior mental powers. Having brought a young female subject totally under his influence, he ultimately uses this control to bring about her death.

Hawthorne's sensitivity to the subtle means by which strong individuals invariably coerce those around them made him wary of mesmerism's moral implications. When his fiancée proposed trying mesmerism as a cure for her headaches he wrote: ". . . my spirit is moved to talk to thee today about these magnetic miracles, and to beseech thee to take no part in them. . . . Supposing that this power arises from the transformation of one spirit into another, it seems to me that the sacredness of an individual is violated by it, there would be an intrusion into thy holy of holies."[31]

This concern carried over into *The Blithedale Romance.* Poking fun at his former Brook Farm compatriots, Hawthorne faulted contemporary philanthropists with forcing their overly intellectual schemes upon society while never actually responding to the concrete needs of actual persons. Hawthorne was able to parody this separation of the intellect from the heart further by adding a subplot in which a mesmerist schemes to use his powers to gain control over an unsuspecting young woman. The book's narrative indicates that Hawthorne was able to assume that his readership was at least partially familiar with mesmerism and the phenomena alleged to occur to subjects in the mesmeric state. One character related instances of the miraculous power of one human being over the will and powers of another. . . . Human character was but soft wax in his hands; and guilt or virtue only the forms into which he should see fit to mold it. . . . It is unutterable, the horror and disgust with which I listened, and saw that . . . the individual soul was virtually annihilated, and all that is sweet and pure in our present life debased.[32]

Hawthorne proved mesmerism to be a literary device capable of engaging his readers' fascination; Edgar Allen Poe perfected its use so as to exacerbate them into a frenzy. Poe devoted himself to studying popular tracts on the subject. On several occasions he observed subjects being placed into the magnetic condition, and he also witnessed a mesmeric séance performed by the renowned spiritualist Andrew Jackson Davis. From Davis he learned that the magnetizing process might enable the finite mind to elevate beyond the physical realm and gain access to esoteric mysteries of the universe. Poe later caricatured these ecstatic flights of the soul in his short story entitled "Mesmeric Revelations." The story opens with an even-tempered review of the facts commonly attributed to the science of mesmerism. The narrator assures his readers that "whatever doubt may still envelop the rationale of mesmerism, its startling facts are now almost universally admitted."[33] We are then treated to an intricate description of how the principal character of the story is voluntarily mesmerized by his good friend. An experienced trance subject, his organs of physical sensation slowly fade from consciousness, thereby enabling his inner faculties to receive direct impressions from that luminiferous ether—animal magnetism. Using what he had learned from Davis concerning the use of the magnetic state for garnering occult and esoteric knowledge, Poe tells that those present begin to interrogate the mesmerized subject concerning secrets of the universe and the key to personal immortality. From his state of superior lucidity, the subject is able to extemporaneously lecture upon numerous subjects of cosmological interest. Of paramount importance is his discovery that animal magnetism constitutes the metaphysical link between the material and spiritual realms of the universe and forms the medium through which the mind must travel upon death in order to obtain to an immortal spiritual state.

Yet another short story "Mesmerism in Articulo Mortis" (later to be known as "The Facts in the Case of M. Valdemar") was a deliberate attempt to push the gullibility of his reading audience to the limit. In this tale Poe again has his main character turn to mesmerism in quest of immortality. Only this time it is not an intellectual curiosity which is to be fulfilled. Knowing that he is dying, M. Valdemar requests a friend to put him into a mesmeric trance, hoping that he might in this way connect himself with the magnetic ethers and enhance his ability to attain immortal life. Horror upon horror, this diabolic deed only traps Valdemar's soul within his now lifeless body. For months on end he remains in an agonized condition at the twilight of death. At long last a friend comes to the rescue by de-mesmerizing him, at which point his body instantly decomposes into "a mass of loathsome—of detestable putridity."[34]

Circulated in an American literary magazine in the mid-1840s, "Mesmerism in Articulo Mortis" created widespread controversy. Its readers were appalled by the blasphemous deeds. Debates raged over the factuality of Poe's story and, if it were true, what should be done to put a stop to the practice of mesmerism. In the words of Elizabeth Barrett Browning, this story which was "going the rounds of the newspapers, about mesmerism, [is] throwing us all into most admired disorder or dreadful doubts as to whether it can be true."[35] Newspapers and magazines were inundated with letters from readers demanding assurance that Poe's account was wholly fictional. Poe wryly refused to comment, but was reported to have enjoyed the furor immensely.

These and other such exploitations of mesmerism had a twofold effect upon popular opinion. On the one hand they impressed popular understandings of animal magnetism with a sense of the diabolical and sinister. Mesmerism was never able to fully expunge these insinuations of witchcraft and black magic. Even into the 1890s Mary Baker Eddy would think it fit to bring lawsuits against those she suspected of practicing "Malicious Animal Magnetism." Educated and sophisticated persons were predisposed to dismiss its theories as, at best, charlatanry and, at worst, a perverse form of the satanic arts. New adherents to mesmerism were henceforth compelled to invent neologisms such as *psychodunamy, psycheism,* or *electrical psychology* to avoid jaundiced reactions to their theories.[36]

At the same time, the public controversy created a readership of a more rational persuasion. Newspapers and magazines devoted space to mesmerists seeking to correct popular distortions of their mental science. Necessity became the mother of clarification, and American mesmerists quickly set about distinguishing their science from aberrant interpretations.

LaRoy Sunderland, for example, launched an immediate counteroffensive against the magnetizer whose "confessions" had damaged mesmerism's moral reputation. Sunderland had been referred to by name in this pamphlet and, though his honor had not been directly impugned, the association alone warranted reply. He denounced the accusations of this wayward scoundrel as so much folly and falsehood. He preferred to regain honor for himself and his theories by once more recounting the long list of mesmerism's positive contributions. Sunderland claimed to have personally magnetized more than fifteen hundred patients. The cures brought relief to those suffering from rheumatism; loss of voice; stammering; nervousness; epilepsy; blindness; insomnia; St. Vitus's Dance; and the abuse of coffee, tobacco, and intoxicating drinks. To be sure, Sundlerland also reaffirmed how experiments with the magnetic condition had led to the discovery of a "sense in man which perceives the presences and qualities of things without the use of either of the external organs of sense."[37] Experiments with the magnetic state had made a giant breakthrough in the conceptualization of the human brain. They proved that, although clairvoyance was "rarely developed in any considerable degree in most patients," it must yet be considered a natural possibility of the nervous system. In order to distinguish these positive contributions from less-lofty pursuits, Sunderland avoided using the term *animal magnetism* whenever possible. He preferred to use the word *Pathetism,* so as to characterize mesmerism more accurately as the science of mental sympathy.

More works appeared with the intention of clarifying mesmerism's empirical foundations. They were, for the most part, highly repetitive. Each began with seemingly

39

endless preliminaries which attempted to remove objections to the subject matter. A short history of Mesmer's discoveries, a cataloging of typical cures accompanied by testimonies from respected medical physicians, and documented reports of clairvoyance and direct thought transference were all standard fare. The most widely circulated work was written by the English magnetizer Reverend Chauncy Townshend. His *Facts in Mesmerism* (1844) became the unofficial canon for the American mesmerists in their attempt to offer what would pass as a philosophical rationale for their observations. Townshend's writings signaled an increasingly bold effort to translate mesmerism into a psychological science. He argued that a "rational and dispassionate inquiry into mesmerism" must begin by eschewing Mesmer's clumsy theories about physical fluids. In their place he offered what could be described as a phenomenological science anchored in the introspective data furnished by mesmerized subjects. Townshend insisted that the proper object of investigation wasn't animal magnetism but rather the unique state of consciousness commonly referred to as the mesmeric state. The conditions and properties of this mental state should be described in their own right, without the unnecessary imposition of laws and principles applicable to physical reality.

Townshend's efforts proved to have important and long-lasting consequences. Mesmerists had already begun to realize that persons vary as to their degree of susceptibility to animal magnetism. With Townshend's help they were now in a position to explain these differences in terms of an individual's psychological constitution rather than the physical properties of animal magnetism. They were also in a better position to speak of continuities between the normal waking state and the magnetic state. In fact, Townshend had demonstrated that, with repeated opportunities, everyone had the ability to achieve some independence from habitual mental states and experience at least the initial stages of the mesmerizing process. Mesmerism amounted to a technique for moving awareness along a continuum which began with ordinary sense perception and led toward a point where entirely new ranges of experience emerged into consciousness. One rendition of Townshend's theory had it that the human system was comprised of four divisions: (1) the material body; (2) the vital, animating principle (animal magnetism); (3) mental powers; and (4) a soul or spirit.[38] According to this schema, when the vital animal magnetic fluids were properly activited, the spirit or inner sense was relieved of its ordinary preoccupation with bodily functions and was temporarily free to enjoy sensations emanating from a more sublime level of reality.

An important implication of this new explanatory model was that the ordinary person was, by definition, constitutionally blinded from acknowledging the realities to which mesmerism attested. The mesmerists could now rest content, knowing that their detractors were arguing from ignorance. Those who pointed to the practitioners of inane stage hypnotism were referring to persons who had never advanced beyond the most superficial levels of the mesmeric state. Persons chasing imaginary canaries at the suggestion of an operator were de facto not in the condition of extraordinary lucidity and, hence, could neither contribute to nor detract from a systematic science of the mind's interior constitution.[39]

Townshend's model implied that those in the magnetic state had gained an interior rapport with levels of reality far more sublime than are available to the average person. It was, thus, natural that the notion of a psychological "continuum" gave way to a "hierarchy." The mesmeric state of consciousness was heralded as the "deepest" and/ or "highest" mental state, depending on whether the analogy was with the inward transition of awareness or the resultant exaltation of mental faculties.[40]

A consensus as to the demarcating properties of the mesmeric state rapidly emerged in the movement's literature.[41] Following Townshend's lead, the mesmerizing process was understood to progress through a series of relatively distinct stages. The initial stage is marked by what today is referred to as a loss of reality orientation. The subject no longer reflects back upon his experience, but rather accepts it at its most literal or nonsymbolic level. Self-consciousness gradually gives way in favor of an ego-less surrender to the present moment. This is often accompanied by the pleasant sensations of spontaneity, freedom from inhibitions, and pervasive contentment. The subject's awareness continues to be preoccupied with inward sensations to the point where, with the single exception of the operator's voice, he soon feels completely impervious to external sensations.

As external stimuli steadily fade from the field of consciousness, wholly new ranges of experience become possible. Or, as Townshend put it, mesmerism brings about "the inaction of the external operations of the sense, coexistent with the life and activity of some inner source of feeling."[42] This inner source of feeling is capable of detecting orders of sensation never monitored by the physical senses. Some persons report feeling alternating warm and cold currents across their bodies; others "see" (though with their eyes closed) flickering rays of light or experience prickly sensations throughout their nervous systems. These sensations were, of course, all attributed to the influx of animal magnetism into their nervous systems.

If the presence of animal magnetism could be palpably detected, its effects were even more apparent. In Mesmer's own words, direct contact with these vital fluids could "immediately cure illness of the nerves and mediately all others." Animal magnetism's sanative powers proved no less potent for the American mesmerists, who amassed an impressive list of medical accomplishments. Their recorded successes were, moreover, backed with affidavits from physicians attesting to their former patients' miraculous recoveries upon undergoing mesmeric treatment. Doubts which the modern might have concerning the accuracy of the diagnoses or the permanency of any alleged relief are, of course, probably unresolvable.[43] But what is certain is the fact that literally thousands believed animal magnetism to be the sole agent responsible for their recovery from heart disease, epilepsy, inflamed joints, rheumatism, recurrent headaches, nervous disorders, menstrual aches, and general melancholia.[44] Cases concerning the mesmeric cure of the lame, deaf, or blind were less common but, nonetheless, accepted as canonical within the mesmerists' literature.[45]

Although instant healings were certainly the principal benefit attributable to what Townshend termed the "inner source of feeling," they were certainly not the only one. Many persons picked up the magnetic streams created by

43

the force of the operator's own thoughts and, in so doing, forged a telepathic bond between them. One magnetizer explained that, concomitant with entrance into these higher levels of the magnetic state, subjects begin to feel

> . . . the irresistible effect of a superior mental power operating upon them, often in spite of their resistance. In the magnetic subject this attraction is produced directly . . . because the mental influence, or the nerve-aura of the operator, controls directly the body of the subject. The phenomena of the animal magnetism depend upon the impressibility of the patient, which renders him susceptible of those delicate influences not felt by others.[46]

He went on to say that he was acquainted with several persons whose "mental sympathy" spontaneously gave them the "power of diagnosis or detection of character, of disease, and of thoughts." And what is more, they could often perform these feats at a distance of many miles.[47] A privileged few managed to transcend the strictures of time and space altogether. Magnetized subjects often became

> . . . clairvoyant, or capable of seeing objects at any distance, without even the assistance of sympathy [with their operator]; they are prevoyant, or capable of foreseeing future events; and they have also intuitive knowledge as to the thought and characters of persons to whom they direct their attention. . . . In truth, there is no definite limit to the range of their intuitive knowledge [whether] in medicine, mental philosophy, theology, chemistry, geology, etc.[48]

Each stage in the mesmerizing process was thought to correspond to a successively deeper level of the mind. Varying but slightly as to detail, the American mesmerists described at least six distinct levels of psychological reality (though some theorists lumped two or more together to come up with three, four, or five):[49]

1. The normal waking state. In the normal waking state the mind is dependent upon the information supplied by the physical organs of sense.

2. The first stage in the mesmerizing process is essentially that of hypnosis. Thinking becomes relatively abstracted from events in the external world. The mind is centered solely on the "suggestions" supplied to it by the operator. All behavior is mechanistically determined by these suggestions with little forethought or consideration of consequences. At this stage of the trance, the subject appears to be uninhibited by his physical or social surroundings and responds only to the operator's suggestions—whether spoken or unspoken.

3. A stage of total insensibility to external sensation. Thought follows its own course irrespective of external conditions. Even the voice of the operator is no longer attended to. This deeper level of the mind appears to be quite independent of, almost impervious to, events occurring in the outer world. Surgical operations have been performed on subjects sufficiently mesmerized to enter this level of consciousness.

4. Catalepsy. Rigidity of the muscles. All but the involuntary functions of the physical organism appear to shut down. It is as if the mind is withdrawing from bodily life altogether.

5. A stage of expanded interior perception. At this level, alleged to be deeper than ordinary hypnosis can reveal, organs of interior perception are said to become active. At this level, the mind is open to impressions coming directly from the environment without reliance upon the five physical senses. Subjects who attain this stage often report tingling sensations or vibrations flow-

ing through them. They often claim to experience waves of energy and to see thin streams of colored light surrounding and emanating from other persons—especially the operator. Healings quite frequently occur as a consequence of this intensified receptivity to vital energies. This level of consciousness is also one in which telepathy, clairvoyance, and other feats of extrasensory perception are said to be possible.

6. A final stage of lucidity or clairvoyant wisdom. Here the individual has come into direct contact with animal magnetic fluid, and his mind is temporarily imbued with its omnipresent and omniscient properties. At this deepest level of consciousness, subjects feel themselves to be united with the creative principle of the universe (animal magnetism). There is a mystical sense of intimate rapport with the cosmos. Subjects feel that they are in possession of knowledge which transcends that of physical, space-time reality. Those who enter this state are able to use it for diagnosing the nature and causes of physical illness. They are also able to exert control over these magnetic healing energies so as to cure persons even at a considerable physical distance. Telepathy, cosmic consciousness, and mystical wisdom, all belong to this deepest level of consciousness discovered in the mesmerists' experiments.

The science of animal magnetism had, in the very process of its Americanization, undergone a successive transformation. It was now less a system of medical healing than a schema demonstrating how the individual mind can establish rapport with ever more sublime levels of reality. Mesmerism was rapidly expanding into a psychologically based pneumatology. That is, it promised to help its adherents transcend the affairs of mundane existence and experience ecstatic states of consciousness and paranormal mental powers. It now remained for the American mesmerists to convince the general public that psychological theories, as opposed to philosophical or theological ones, had sufficient relevance to their moral and intellectual interests to warrant further consideration.

Chapter 3

The Emergence of an American Psychology

It is a well known fact that mesmerism gives striking invigoration and exaltation to the intellectual and moral faculties . . . it seems scarcely possible that [it] could fail to become a moral and religious engine of great power and value.
—*Charles Caldwell, 1842*

By the mid 1840s the American mesmerists had succeeded in fully isolating themselves in a cultural no man's land. Their discoveries had led them so deeply into unchartered territories that they no longer knew where they belonged. Neither the medical nor physical sciences were prepared to embrace subjective phenomena as empirical data. The so-called facts of mesmerism weren't really facts at all. Nor were sizeable numbers of America's pragmatic middle class as yet ready to take its testimonies concerning paranormal mental powers very seriously. The testimonies simply contradicted common sense. And besides, who cared? The discoveries were of no possible use to anyone too busy to be rendered comatose by some itinerant stranger.

48

Mesmerism found itself supplying a remedy for which there was as yet no known deficiency. Which is to say it had no consumer value. The next several years in its growth in the United States reveal how very dependent theories, particularly psychological theories, are upon their ability to satisfy the conceptual needs of the general populace. Yet the subsequent directions taken by this early psychology record the initial stages of the emergence of our modern social sciences. For, as it turns out, the mesmerists' theories were at the forefront of the intellectual revolution during which religious or theological forms of self-understanding were steadily abandoned in favor of those more in keeping with a modern, secular world.

The American mesmerists never fully recognized the ideological dimensions of their efforts to account for man's inner life in strictly scientific terms. As a consequence, their writings often made a fine art of fuzzy thinking. Unable to decide whether psychology should be considered an extension of physiology or metaphysics, the mesmerists chose to blur the distinctions between the two. A few decades later, a more scientific psychology would thoroughly dispose of the quasi-religious considerations which the mesmerists deemed important to understanding human nature. But in the meantime it was their very reluctance to make hard and fast distinctions between sacred and secular which enabled them to investigate psychological issues without thinking themselves to be undermining traditional religious values. Mesmerism's location midway between the religious and scientific paradigms competing for the allegiance of nineteenth-century Americans made psychological ideas appear as a way of shifting, not eradicating, traditional categories of self-understanding.

The only other psychological theory with which Americans were as yet acquainted was phrenology. Also of European origin, phrenology made a less circuitous passage across the Atlantic and arrived nearly a decade before Poyen.[1] We have already noted that Robert Collyer began his lecture circuit to popularize the merits of phrenology only to find his audience more responsive to mesmerism. His was not an isolated case. Mesmerism quickly overshadowed its only predecessor, and the reasons are most instructive.

Phrenology amounted to the topographical division of the brain into innumerable compartments or faculties. Since each faculty was assumed to be the physiological center of a distinct personality trait, the relative size of any particular area of a person's skull was considered a reliable indication of their character. In due time every conceivable moral and intellectual disposition was accorded its own anatomical location. Unfortunately, no one quite knew what to do with these detailed inventories. An employer might decide to give preference to a job candidate with a pronounced bump in his region of frugality, but that was about the extent of it.

More-inventive applications were occasionally proposed. It was suggested that leeches could be placed on criminals' heads so as to siphon off the strength from their faculties of deceit and larceny. Some phrenologists prescribed mental exercises. Memorizing pithy maxims was believed to stimulate growth in otherwise underdeveloped sections of the brain. Yet when all was said and done, phrenology remained a system of classification. Its efforts to spawn self-improvement programs were so wedded to a physiological materialism that they appeared discouragingly futile. As one phrenologist-turned-mesmerist remarked, even the most vigorous exercising of the phreno organs couldn't make a Franklin of a Hottentot in a single generation.

Phrenology's swift exit from the American intellectual scene was not dictated by any full-scale refutation of its theories. Few rigorous physiological or psychological arguments were ever raised against it. For that matter, Americans had no alternative theories to counterpose. Phrenology's failure was, in the last analysis, one of ideology. Its master image of human personality was incompatible with the pragmatic temper of the American people and the religiomoral assumptions which sustained it. A physiological explanation of moral character forces one to accept the concept that personality is rigidly determined by inherited brain organs. This would never hold up under the scrutiny of American audiences. They knew proper conduct to be a far more volitional achievement. Most knew it to be a direct consequence of firm religious belief. Infidels, no matter how well developed their skulls, were forever suspect in a predominantly Puritan New England. One observer astutely reasoned that phrenology's materialistic assumptions ultimately implied "a world without souls" and, worse yet, "without God."[2] Phrenology, he continued, was guilty of unmitigated atheism. Even though it postulated organs of worship, reverence, and so forth, it made no provisions as to what object these faculties ought rightfully to be directed.

Most Americans had been brought up to consider human nature, precisely on account of its corporeal composition, to be base. The mind needed to be made over, not developed. The value of religion in general and of the phenomenon of conversion in particular was that they elevated the mind above corporality to a higher spiritual state. A distinct inward transformation was thought to be both logically and ontologically prior to authentic self-improvement. And while the Protestant ethic is an elusive entity upon which to rest historical judgments, it seems fair to generalize that a felt-sense of the divine ranked high in the period's conception of the good and successful individual. The closest phrenology came to accommodating these cultural assumptions was to make room for faculties of veneration, worship, and the like. But even if these venerable faculties could be multiplied indefinitely, the phrenological conception of human nature would still have left Americans cold. They wouldn't settle for a theory of man's mental constitution which neglected its capacity to become a vessel of the Holy Spirit. Phrenology never made sufficient allowance for the wider cultural ethos—and suffered the consequences.

American phrenologists took an early interest in mesmerism, hoping that it would assist them in their efforts to make more-precise craniological charts. Investigators believed that they could eliminate extraneous influences by putting subjects into a light trance before they set about pressing their hands against various portions of the head. By observing the subjects' subsequent behaviors, they believed they could pinpoint the exact location of each major phrenological faculty. Unfortunately, phrenomagnetism accomplished little more than the provocation of irresolvable arguments between investigators whose findings, not surprisingly, contradicted one another. The *American Phrenological Journal* followed these debates with waning enthusiasm before concluding that phrenomagnetism was ineradicably plagued with "speculative inferences."

It was only natural that many who dabbled in phrenomagnetism soon became enamored of the magnetic state in its own right. It revealed mental life to be much more dynamic and susceptible to thoroughgoing improvements than the phrenological system had allowed for. As one phrenomagnetist concluded, "Without magnetism phrenology is no more than a body without a soul. For what is the brain or its various developments, without life?"[3]

One of the first to recognize mesmerism's advantages over phrenological understandings of the brain was Dr. Joseph Buchanan. A medical school professor of physiology, Buchanan credited mesmerism with establishing the neurological principle of impressibility. The mesmerists' experiments demonstrated that the outside world constantly impresses information upon the brain. Furthermore, they revealed two quite distinct means by which sensations enter into our consciousness. The first is that of physical impressibility, or the brain's neurological response to information supplied by the five physical senses. Studies of the mesmerizing process showed the brain to be an active agent in constant rapport with the surrounding environment. This alone constituted a theoretical advance over phrenology's static characterization of self-contained mental organs.

Prior to the discovery of the mesmeric state, physical impressibility was the only means of sensation recognized by neurological science. But mesmerism had come upon the startling discovery that the mind is also susceptible to spiritual or nonphysical sensations. Buchanan referred to this second type of brain activity as "mental impressibility."[4]

Clairvoyance and telepathy were proof that the mind is capable of gaining information about the world without any dependence upon the physical senses. It is not altogether clear how Buchanan believed the doctrine of mental impressibility affected neurology's status as either a medical or physical science, but he did draw attention to the fact that it forged a conceptual synthesis of man's physical and spiritual natures. Mental impressibility provided him and other early American psychologists with a "key to the whole science of Anthropology. It gives us a dynamic anthropology—psychological and physiological."[5]

Buchanan was not alone in thinking that psychology was the most appropriate area in which to develop a comprehensive theory of human nature. Now armed with a doctrine of spiritual influence, psychology promised to bring the physical, mental, and religious spheres of man's existence into a single conceptual framework. First, however, it remained for mesmerists to expand their observations into a comprehensive psychological doctrine. J. Stanley Grimes put the charge in as muddled terms as any when he declared it incumbent upon his fellow mesmerists to prove "the extraordinary phenomena of nature as all explicable by the irregularity of the same causes which produce the regular."[6]

The mesmerists' efforts to construct a general psychology were clumsy, to say the least. They had inherited a theory that described the structures of psychological reality in the jargon of contemporary physics. It was only gradually that they were able to educe a more fully psychological perspective from their observations of magnetized subjects. The first problem they faced was deciding whether the mesmeric state was produced by intrapersonal or extrapersonal variables. Unable to accept the consequences of either, they took a safer route and chose both. An article that appeared in *Buchanan's Journal of Man* in 1849 registers the confusion:

The established fact, that imagination may effect the most wonderful cures . . . seems to have been overlooked by the early magnetizers; they could see nothing in all their experiments but the potency of the wonderful and mysterious "fluid." On the other hand, the anti-mesmeric party, knowing the powers of the imagination, were blind to the existence of any other agent. . . . It is probable that, in this matter, both the mesmerizers and their opponents were wrong in the ultra and exclusive doctrine which each party maintained—but with the lapse of time, we now see that each party had progressed nearer the truth. The opponents of animal magnetism have yielded by thousands to the conviction, that there are forces of some kind emitted by the human constitution which had not been recognized in their philisophy; and, on the other hand, many mesmerizers (in the United States at least) have learned that many of their most interesting results are really the product of imagination.[7]

The American mesmerists were awakening to the fact that their experiments attested to an autonomous psychological realm. Well aware of the role that "suggestion" (i.e., the subject's tendency to subconsciously comply with the operator) and prior expectations played in determining the behavior of a person in the magnetic state, mesmerists became the first Americans to directly study the psychodynamic nature of interpersonal relationships. Not that their insights were particularly perspicacious. Poyen picked up the scent when it dawned upon him that he had not once encountered a subject who could clairvoyantly describe scenes of a city which he had not previously visited. It became obvious to him that a somnambule must already have the appropriate sense perceptions in his head if he is to mentally zero in on specific streets or houses. Befuddled as to just what his observation implied, he concluded that "such a thing is inexplicable and cannot be referred to any philosophical principle."[8] Sunderland ventured a bit further when he proposed that the mental influence which a mesmeric operator wields over an entranced subject is not due to some external agency (animal magnetism), but is rather on a continuum with the influence one mind always has over another.[9]

Although it took him several decades to do so, J. Stanley Grimes went the furthest of all American mesmerists in discarding physicalistic interpretations of the magnetic state of consciousness.[10] Picking up on the earlier suggestions of a British physician by the name of William Carpenter,[11] Grimes argued that the behaviors of entranced subjects were largely the products of unintentional self-deception. Most, if not all, of these strange phenomena could be reduced to the subject's subdued will and abnormally active propensities for imitativeness, credenciveness, believing, and above all—conforming. Interestingly, Grimes never repudiated the "reality" of the evidence which he had personally garnered in support of telepathy and clairvoyance.

Most American mesmerists, however, were by no means convinced that the "imagination" or "suggestibility" could account for their data. They feared that without the admission of animal magnetism, however loosely interpreted, their theory quite literally lacked substance. A purely subjective psychological reality was beyond their conceptual horizons. And for that matter, it couldn't be supported on the basis of the data furnished by their magnetized patients. Those who entered into the highest degree of the mesmeric state detected the existence of a discrete and even palpable force impinging upon their nervous systems from without. Thus the American mesmerists weren't disposed toward pursuing the phenomenon of suggestion as relentlessly as were their later European counterparts. It was left to Charcot, Breuer, Janet, and, finally, Freud to follow this enigmatic creature until arriving at the foundations of dynamic psychiatry. Their entranced patients displayed mental behaviors which aroused numerous suspicions about the subconscious reaches of the mind. Psychoanalysis eventually revealed how mankind's subjective life, far from glorifying human nature, actually distorts it. A superior psychology perhaps, but its data base was far too narrow for the mesmerists. The psychoanalysts believed that the subconscious mind was totally incarcerated by the perceptions of the finite ego. The mesmerists insisted, to the contrary, that an individual's "inner source of feeling" opens the finite mind to transpersonal domains.

Most American mesmerists continued to believe that any theoretical advances would come by refining, not abandoning, Mesmer's doctrine of animal magnetism. And, oddly enough, the development of neurophysiology in the United States owes a debt to the mesmerists' efforts to discover the physiological mechanisms through which animal magnetism influences human consciousness. Convinced that their observations could be accounted for within a suitably enlarged science, the mesmerists offered

57

as detailed neurophysiological explanations as contemporary medical research permitted. Several investigators advanced the notion that the electrical impulses in the human nervous system are the physiological form taken by animal magnetism when it enters the human nervous system. For instance, John Dods proposed that in the act of breathing the body absorbs animal magnetism in its original, rarefied state and transforms it into nervo-vital fluid.[12] In another version, the brain itself was said to secrete this marvelous substance.[13] LaRoy Sunderland tried a slightly different tack when he postulated the existence of two distinct brain organs, each housing one of the two alternating forces of life.[14] He argued that one brain coordinates incoming sensory information with appropriate reactions by the voluntary muscles. The other is responsible for the involuntary functions of the nervous system and acts upon information it receives independently of the five physical senses. It followed that the normal waking state of consciousness is characterized by the predominance of the external senses and voluntary nervous system, while the magnetic state is one in which the second brain temporarily functions as the dominant mode of awareness.

However, it must be pointed out that the mesmerists were every bit as reluctant to follow a neurophysiological perspective to its logical conclusion as they were a psychodynamic one. The phenomena of direct thought transference, clairvoyance, prevision, and mystical rapture could not be properly accounted for with reference to a neuro-electrical force constrained within the brain. The same writer who, in one connection, insisted that animal magnetism is a substance effused by the brain to carry messages throughout the nervous system was equally certain that the "doctrine of animal magnetism is the connecting link between physiology and psychology . . . it demonstrates the intimate interconnection between the natural and the spiritual."[15] The terms *spiritual* and *psychological* were by now completely interchangeable in the mesmerists' vocabulary. Each referred to the fact that the mind was, in some fundamental respect, irreducible to physical conditions.

As awkward as all of this appears, the mesmerists were quite incapable of striking out in any other direction. They were merely trying to account for psychological reality in the language used by popular tracts to explain other invisible realities, such as electricity, gravitation, and magnetism. In the early 1850s a two-volume *Library of Mesmerism and Psychology* appeared, consisting of articles submitted by several of the movement's preeminent spokesmen.[16] The work is notable only for the fact that its authors apparently found it much easier to reach general accord on highly abstract cosmological doctrines than on factors influencing human consciousness. Their theoretical efforts were wedded to the same narrow views of reality and scientific empiricism as were Mesmer's twenty-seven principles. A science of the mind was, by definition, possible only by postulating an identity between the human nervous system and the magnetic medium now "known" to transmit sensations in the material universe. The nature of the mind, as microcosm, could be rationally inferred only from the metaphysical operations of the macrocosm.

Townshend struggled with the problem of evidencing the objective reality of mental life for some time before concluding that "the electrical force, then, will naturally occur to him who seeks a penetrating and pervading medium, as resolvable of the enigma of mesmerism."[17] The recent scientific discovery of electricity thoroughly baffled nineteenth-century Americans anyway; once adopted as an explanatory device by the mesmerists, almost any degree of ambiguity could pass muster. Soon John Dods was referring to mesmerism as the philosophy of electrical psychology. In his writings the word *electricity* became a metaphor for the power of an invisible agent to produce actual effects in the material world. J. Stanley Grimes coined yet another scientific-sounding neologism for animal magnetism—*the etherium.* Grimes proposed that the etherium is a "material substance occupying space, which connects the planets and the earth, and which communicates light, heat, electricity, gravitation, and mental emanations one body to another and from one mind to another."[18] This would all be fine if Grimes, a professor of medical jurisprudence, were merely engaging in cosmological speculation. But he was propounding etherology as a "phreno-philosophy of mesmerism, and magic eloquence, including a new philosophy of sleep and of consciousness."

Whereas Mesmer had intended his theory to show how both medical and nonmedical healings were but variations of the selfsame principle, its Yankee counterpart was thought to explain the commonalities between normal and transcendent states of consciousness. The hierarchical model of mind/brain interaction which Townshend and others proposed made it possible to speak of the existence of levels of consciousness structurally distinct from that of the normal waking state. But, at the same time, this model cast doubt on the validity of strictly psychological explanations of human nature. Psychodynamic and neurophysiological insights into the nature of the mind pertained only to one of several possible levels of psychological reality. As explanatory concepts, therefore, they pinpointed only the material or efficient causes of mental phenomena such as those which occur in the magnetic state. That is, factors such as suggestion or impressibility merely account for why a person's awareness shifts along the continuum of conscious sensation. But the final or ultimate cause of the resultant elevation of consciousness belongs to a metaphysical, not metapsychological, system of explanation.

The confusion as to the exact nature of psychological reasoning was compounded by the fact that mesmerism appeared fifty years before the establishment of the first department of psychology at an American university. The mesmerists' theories were thus formulated outside of any institutional setting. They consequently lacked the kind of specialized focus which collegiality, corroborative research, and professional associations impart to a theoretical discipline. The audience to which the mesmerists addressed their theories was the general public. It would be inappropriate, then, to expect mesmerist psychology to have developed in accordance with the kinds of criteria identified by disinterested scientific observers. A psychological theory attracts a popular following, not by virtue of its formal scientific status, but rather by promising practical solutions to problems which arise in the context of everyday life. The path followed by a "popular psychology" is, for this reason, hewn by the very needs and interests which it endeavors to satisfy. The American mesmerists were able to win over a constituency only by demonstrating the ways in which their theories were applicable to the vital issues of the day. The process through which these early psychological ideas first entered into American cultural thought can be reconstructed at least in part with reference to the writings of the midwestern physician Charles Caldwell.

Caldwell makes for a fascinating point of entry into the early history of American psychology for a number of reasons. First, he was without question one of his generation's leading medical authorities. He had studied for his medical degree at the University of Pennsylvania under the direction of Benjamin Rush and later helped found the Midwest's first medical school at Transylvania College. Second, Caldwell's moral and religious dispositions are sufficiently well known to help clarify the reasons for his interest in psychological ideas.[19] A brief glance at the history of American psychology shows that an inordinately large percentage of its early founders were either sons of Protestant ministers or seriously entertained notions of entering the ministry themselves. Caldwell's father, while not a minister, was a devout elder in the Presbyterian church and exerted considerable pressure on his son to enroll in the seminary. Charles resisted in favor of a career more in keeping with his conviction that true religion consisted not in doctrinal speculation but rather in philanthropic activity. His was to be a career dedicated to alleviating concrete needs through the practice of medicine and to championing progressivist social causes. In publications that totaled over twelve thousand pages, he gave vocal support to a number of liberal reforms ranging from abolition to free public education.

Foremost amongst Caldwell's ideological crusades was his attempt to bring scientific understandings of human nature to bear upon moral and religious issues. As early as 1839 he had written a monograph entitled "Thoughts on the True Connexion of Phrenology and Religion."[20] This article directly linked Americans' first interest in psychology with the "religion versus science" debate which, over the course of several decades, crystallized the nation's intellectual confrontation with modernity. Caldwell endorsed phrenology because it offered a nonevangelical theory of "the duty which we owe to ourselves, to society and to a still Higher Power of so cultivating and disciplining our minds as to give . . . our moral and intellectual nature the supremacy over our animal."[21] Phrenological psychology supported the individual's progressive moral development while freeing him from the heteronomous authority of revealed religion. Knowledge of the mind and its powers would also provide individuals with a set of rational criteria for choosing which religious doctrines are most compatible with human progress.

His book *Facts in Mesmerism* extended Caldwell's early thoughts into a full-fledged manifesto. His introductory remarks neatly placed the facts of mesmerism in their proper cultural context. The Christian religion was, in his opinion, becoming increasingly irrelevant. Its irrational features were so untenable in light of scientific advancements that many intellectuals had come to reject religion altogether. Caldwell urged that a wholesale abandonment was unnecessary. Religion needed only to be purged "of its false doctrines and teachings, superstitions and extravagances, and employed in its genuine principles for the improvement of man and the amelioration of his condition."[22]

The spiritual purgative Caldwell had in mind was the

"facts in mesmerism." For a medical physician Caldwell devoted surprisingly little attention to mesmerism's curative powers. It seems that the facts, or at least the important ones, were those that dealt with the paranormal phenomena associated with the mesmeric state. These phenomena impressed Caldwell as giving "some antepast of the existence and character of mind or spirit when separated from the body."[23] Mesmerism's vivid description of man's higher nature reinforced the essential percepts of revealed religion even if in doing so they recast them in a more naturalistic light. Its psychological theories showed ecstatic states of mind to be thoroughly lawful and thus consonant with rational control. At last religion was being distilled to its genuine principles.

Dr. Caldwell predictably hailed mesmerism's contributions before the medical community. Its techniques promised to bring entirely new ranges of mental and nervous disorders under the jurisdiction of medical science. But Caldwell recognized that the study of the mind had more than remedial import. It also gave hints about what man can and ought to be. "It is a well known fact," he claimed, "that mesmerism gives striking invigoration and exaltation to the intellectual and moral faculties . . . [it] augments their strength, improves their habits of action and thus aids in bestowing on them that control over their lower faculties in which consists the most virtuous and useful condition of the mind."[24] It was, therefore, the clergy who stood to benefit most from the facts in mesmerism. Caldwell exhorted that "if skillfully and vigorously wielded by them it seems scarcely possible that mesmerism could fail to become a moral and religious engine of great power and value."[25]

Whether he knew it or not, Caldwell was selling psychology to an American consumer market. He identified pervasive cultural needs and demonstrated his product's ability to meet them. In the process Caldwell was inflating this psychological system into a blueprint for personal and social innovation. His conviction that psychological ideas permitted of widespread application was soon reinforced by another midwesterner, Joseph Buchanan.[26]

Buchanan's lifelong ambition was to create a new branch of science which he called "neurological anthropology." He had in mind nothing less than bringing all the disparate facts of human nature together into one holistic framework. Medical science, philosophy, and religion were all to be taken into account. This was to be no mean task for a professor of physiology. One of his primary efforts was the *Journal of Man,* which served as a clearing house for articles of possible relevance to his project. Eclecticism proved the better part of discretion in his editorial policies, and the journal quickly degenerated into an encyclopedia of the period's most benighted efforts to put itself in metaphysical perspective.

Buchanan's efforts were consistent in at least one respect. He reasoned that true religion and true science must ultimately be compatible, and it was the purpose of a neurological anthropology to evidence that interconnection. Buchanan wasn't about to restrict mesmerism to its medical utility. To him it was a hermeneutic principle unveiling man's psychosomatic unity. The doctrine of animal magnetism taught that "positive material existence and positive Spiritual existence—however far apart they stand, and however striking the contrast between their properties—are connected by these fine gradations . . . both are subject to the same great system of laws which each obeys in its own sphere."[27]

According to Buchanan, strictly physiological theories of human nature lead inevitably to materialism, pessimism, and atheism. He rejected current medical science as an inadequate framework for describing the human constitution, "since it lacks the essential perspective of the modus operandi of life power."[28] Theological dogma, while recognizing man's higher, spiritual nature, was likewise unacceptable. It undermined the inductive spirit of the whole project. Mesmerist psychology inaugurated an intellectual breakthrough of the highest magnitude. It forged the relative contributions of medical physiology and theology into a higher synthesis. At long last Buchanan could confidently affirm that "the power of disembodied mind and intellectual manifestations . . . fall within the scope of the fundamental principles of the constitution of man, and spiritual mysteries, too, are beautifully elucidated by the complete correspondence, and mathematical harmony, between the spiritual and material laws of our being."[29]

Buchanan fancied that the neurological anthropologist was soon to become one of the most important members of society. He alone would possess the psychological insights to instruct persons about practical virtues. Moreover, "his function is similar to that of the clergyman, and in fact although the anthropologist may not be formally a clergyman, every clergyman should be, for the fulfillment of his own duties, a thorough anthropologist."[30] Buchanan's thinking here resembles the "psychology of religion" movement which emerged a full forty years later. In each case it was thought that the fledgling field of psy-

66

chology could best achieve intellectual autonomy by demonstrating that religious thinking is little more than a disguised psychology.

Buchanan was, by this point, in a position to do what neither phrenologists nor the earlier mesmerists had been capable of doing. He could enumerate the practical applications to which a psychological perspective might be put. And he did; a full seventeen of them. The "practical tendencies and utilities" of mesmerist psychology included a philosophy for self-study and self-improvement; the regulation of social intercourse; education of the young; renovation of society; development of rational therapeutics; renovation of moral philosophy; renovation of theology; expansion of the mind; and a proper pneumatology.[31]

The writings of Caldwell and Buchanan make it clear that psychological science emerged with the surging tide of nineteenth-century optimism and faith in human progress. Like other sciences in this period it, too, promised to harness formerly hidden forces for human use. The laws of psychological science would be but one more means of pushing back all known limits to human progress. John Dods boasted that mesmerism had climbed aboard that "glorious chariot of science with its ever increasing power, magnificence and glory . . . ever obeying the command of God: ONWARD."[32]

The glorious chariot of science had but to follow the course already laid down by the laws of nature, and upward progress was assured. Antebellum Americans considered the empirical method to be perfectly compatible with religious faith. Mesmerism was ample proof that scientific observation would eventually disclose the providential hand of God present throughout nature. Townshend, himself a clergyman, went so far as to describe the mesmeric state as a "boon granted by God to confirm our faith and to cheer us on our way."[33] Mesmerist psychology was but the newest means whereby mankind might discover, and then adjust itself to, the divinely appointed order of things. Its doctrines were interpreted as being a systematic exposition of "how we are constituted, how nearly we are related to, and how far we resemble our original . . . God who is a pure spiritual essence."[34] And though these observed truths might not fall within the letter of Christian Scripture, they certainly reinforced its spirit. Mesmerist psychology was terribly reassuring concerning man's possession of a higher spiritual nature. Dods voiced the majority opinion by drawing attention to the fact that the mesmeric state "shows that man has within him a spiritual nature which can live without the body . . . in the eternal NOW of a future existence."[35]

Thus by the 1850s American mesmerism was straddling a fine line between religious myth and scientific psychology. Neither a psychotherapy nor a sacrament, its healing methods yet seemed to have the dynamics of each. Mesmerism's explanation of human health and happiness held that personal wholeness was not reducible to mechanistic analysis but rather entered into the finite personality from some transpersonal source. The American mesmerists had finally settled upon a psychological doctrine whose chief value was that it reassured individuals that they possessed within themselves the ability to harmonize with what Buchanan called "the modus operandi of life powers." No wonder mesmerism appeared so attractive to those caught up in the currents of religious experimentalism then sweeping across the nation.

68

Chapter 4

Psychology out of Its Mind

*The state into which a subject is brought by the mesmeric process
is a state in which the spirit predominates, for the time being,
over the body.*
—*George Bush, 1847*

The American mesmerists continued to make headway
throughout the late 1830s and early 40s. Although their
efforts to generate a readership for monthly journals met
with little success, they found themselves in great demand
as public lecturers.[1] Collyer, Sunderland, Grimes, and
Dods drew large crowds as they made their New England
rounds. One report casually refers to Sunderland giving
a lecture-demonstration before "some two thousand people, principally composed of the middling classes of the
community."[2] John Dods filled Boston's Marlboro Chapel
with more than two thousand for six nights running.[3]
These lectures were immediately transposed into a book
which proceeded to go through several editions. Dods's
discourses on "the philosophy of mesmerism" evidently
created quite a stir. As word of his controversial theory
spread along the seaboard, several U.S. senators wrote

Dods, requesting that he deliver a similar series of lectures in the nation's capital. Henry Clay, Sam Houston, and Daniel Webster added their names to the list of those voicing interest in what had been described to them as a "new philosophy of disease and the reciprocal action of mind and matter upon each other."[4]

Ironically, mesmerism's hard-fought campaign to earn recognition as a psychological science was, from the outset, destined to go awry. The fact that its ideas were being addressed to popular rather than scientific audiences dictated wholesale changes. A popular psychology will either flourish or literally vanish into thin air, depending on whether some segment of the general public perceives it as having concrete application in their lives. It was, thus, inevitable that mesmerism would gradually forego further theoretical reflection in favor of proffering practical self-help strategies. The biggest single difference between the kinds of reassurances and exhortations which the mesmerists aimed at their audience and those found in modern psychological literature stemmed from the expectations of the clientele itself. In the nineteenth century self-improvement aspirations weren't narrowly focused on isolated behavioral problems like weight control or sexual impotence. Rather, personality change had to do with re-shaping one's entire outlook on life. It involved opening up to some higher level of self-understanding. Thus when Buchanan listed philosophy, theology, and pneumatology foremost among mesmerism's "practical tendencies and utilities," he was merely demonstrating its relevance to the categories within which his contemporaries interpreted their lives.

Nomenclature underwent rapid revision as the mesmerists learned to target their theories more accurately to the cultural marketplace. Dods sensed that the term *animal magnetism* had outlived its usefulness. He thought it more appropriate to portray this new philosophy as "spiritualism" or "the science of the mind and its powers."[5] Joseph Haddock believed there was good reason for describing mesmerism as "the science of the soul considered physiologically and philosophically."[6] Still another proposal called for identifying animal magnetism as the "power of the soul" and "the intelligent principle of life which the deity has conceded to living beings."[7]

These terminological changes had the advantage of at last giving formal recognition to certain features which had been implicit in Americans' interpretation of mesmerism from the start. The act of placing persons into the magnetic state could scarcely have struck American audiences otherwise than as decidedly religious in character. Mesmerism received attention, not because it healed the physical body, but for the more important reason that it effected a change in a person's spiritual outlook on life. By putting individuals into more direct connection with the ontological source of their physical and mental being, mesmerists mobilized those particular emotions which, throughout the course of human history, have manifested themselves in religious ritual. According to anthropologist Arnold van Gennep, cultures everywhere provide ritualized means for assisting individuals through difficult personality adjustments.[8] "Rites of passage" progress through three more or less distinct stages, during which a person's identity is progressively transformed in accordance with the moral and religious beliefs of the larger community. Insofar as the mesmerizing process (1) separated individuals from their accustomed identity, (2) temporarily induced a paranormal state of consciousness understood to be one which imparts a vivid insight into ontological truths otherwise beyond human comprehension, and (3) returned these now experientially invigorated persons to everyday reality armed with new insights into the nature of life, it guided individuals through the very stages which comprise a religious rite of passage.

This structural affinity between mesmerism and religious ritual was without question a crucial factor behind its therapeutic successes. As with rituals generally, the mesmerizing process was thought to require a special setting removed from the hustle and bustle of daily existence. Specific attitudes, or inward dispositions, were called for. The patient was to become silent, self-effacing, and submissive before a healer who was understood to be in special rapport with higher cosmic powers. Mesmerism even had its own psychologized version of the laying on of hands. It was commonly believed that, while the operator passed his hands over the patient, a "substance emanates from him who magnetizes and is conveyed to the person magnetized by the will."[9] Mesmeric passes possessed the power to "reverse, disperse, concentrate, and change the vital forces."[10]

The onset of the mesmeric state of consciousness prepared the patient for an almost sacramental encounter with a transmundane spiritual agent. Contact with this etheric substance momentarily transformed and elevated the patient's very being. A fairly typical account of this encounter related how

the whole moral and intellectual character becomes changed from the degraded condition of earth to the exalted intelligence of a spiritual state. The external senses are all suspended and the internal sense of spirit acts with its natural power as it will when entirely freed from the body after death. No person, we think, can listen to the revelations of a subject in a magnetic state, respecting the mysteries of our nature, and continue to doubt the existence of a never dying soul and the existence of a future or heavenly life.[11]

It is evident that Americans found mesmerism to be treating the whole person rather than isolated complaints. Through this ritualized death and rebirth of the conscious personality, patients believed themselves to be reestablishing inner harmony with the very source of physical and emotional well-being. While in the mesmeric state, they learned that disease and even moral confusion were but the unfortunate consequences of having fallen out of rapport with the invisible spiritual workings of the universe. Conversely, health and personal virtue were the automatic rewards of living in accordance with the cosmic order. When patients returned from their ecstatic mental journey, they knew themselves to have been raised to a higher level of participation in the life-power that "activates the whole frame of nature and produces all the phenomena that transpire throughout the realms of unbounded space."[12]

This entire scenario invoked an explanatory logic which neatly paralleled that given for the single most effective ritual in American religious history—revivalism. For all its peculiarities, mesmerism bore strong resemblances to the religious revivals which, for years, had served as the pre-eminent curator of the national psyche. American Protestantism, with its obsession for saving souls through distinct conversion experiences, created a metaphysical climate which assured mesmerism a receptive audience. The nation's Calvinist theological heritage had fostered a widespread conviction that personal improvements of every kind were possible only through the gracious activity of the Holy Spirit. Thus, individuals who suffered from moral, intellectual, and emotional conflicts desperately hoped for a specific sign of regeneration in the form of a conversion experience. Revivals played upon Americans' doubts concerning the sufficiency of their own personal resources by promising any and all the chance to be literally born anew.

The term *awakening* is generally given to wide-scale outbreaks of revival activity. The First Great Awakening in American religious history lasted from roughly 1730 to 1760. During this period, enterprising preachers staged mass gatherings, or revivals, for the purpose of winning converts to the Christian faith. The fact that thousands were thereby brought to the "conviction of sin" and urged to publicly renew their commitment to Christian teachings permanently altered the tone and substance of American religious thought. Revivalist gatherings proved so effective in dramatizing the baseness of man's lower nature and eliciting a highly emotional encounter with the Holy Spirit that they have been, from that time forth, powerful institutions of both personal and social renewal.

When placed in historical perspective, each new outburst of revivalist activity can be seen to have prefigured innovative developments in American religious thought and practice. Dating back to George Whitefield's early attempt to organize large-scale proselytizing campaigns, revivalist practices and the theories that justify them have existed in a creative tension with the nation's Calvinist theological heritage. Though never willing to hedge on the issue of the "wholly otherness" of God in a manner that would smack of secular humanism (or, in earlier times, deism), the revivalist tradition is yet wedded to the very anti-Calvinist proposition that an individual can take responsible steps toward procuring his own salvation. And, in point of fact, popular American religious thought has never fully succumbed to the Calvinist insistence that the ultimate criteria upon which human actions are to be judged lie beyond the grasp of human reason. Perry Miller has pointed out that, from the outset, American religious thought has been committed to the conviction that "in some fashion the transcendent God had to be chained, made less inscrutable, less mysterious, less unpredictable—He had to be made, again, understandable in human terms."[13] The attempt to make soteriology a more accessible and even convenient affair made for a peculiarly American rendering of the doctrine of a divine covenant. The whole notion that God had entered into a covenant with his creation was interpreted as an assurance that God had fully laid down "the conditions by which Heaven is obtained and he who fulfills the conditions has an incontestable title to glorification."[14] In each successive epoch of American history new variations of revivalism have emerged to reinterpret these covenantal requirements and make them capable of wide-scale application.

Mesmerism's appearance in the mid-1830s coincided with the apogee of the Second Great Awakening. The early nineteenth century was an era of unprecedented self-confidence for the spanking new nation. Boundaries, both intellectual and geographical, were being pushed back with almost startling alacrity. National faith in the manifest destiny of the American people was beginning to receive abundant confirmation. It was in this buoyant setting that what is known as "alleviated Calvinism" first gained ascendancy in American religious thought. The major consequence of this gradual shift in religious temperament was that evangelical religiosity began to gravitate toward an Arminian understanding of the salvation process. The tendency was to view evil no longer as the outward sign of mankind's innate depravity but rather as a function of ignorance, a lack of self-discipline, or a result of faulty social institutions. Man's "lower nature" was, therefore, potentially perfectible through humanly initiated reforms. The optimistic, even utopian, belief in the potential perfectibility of the human condition was thus beginning to redefine the conditions thought indispensable to the fulfillment of human destiny. A new breed of revivalist appeared dedicated to the proposition that human nature is capable of immediate and total renovation. It was not just the opportunity but even the duty of the revivalist preacher to provide a social and psychological environment favorable to an abrupt change of mind and will.

It was Charles Grandison Finney who epitomized the period's changing conception of the origin of human difficulties. His *Lectures on Revivals,* published in 1835, outlined what he believed to be an empirically tested system of techniques ("new measures") designed to turn the conversion process into a lawful science. In Finney's estimation, a conversion "is not a miracle or dependent on a miracle in any sense . . . it consists entirely in the right exercise of the powers of nature."[15] By implication, religious experience can be humanly engineered. His was a scientific

pneumatology predicated on the fact that "God had connected means with ends through all departments of his
government—in nature and in grace."[16] Religious conversions were procured by a scientific application of natural
laws, not a miraculous intervention of them. Believing that
even the most inward of religious experiences had distinct
correlates in the outer world, Finney counseled that "he
who deals with souls should study well the laws of the
mind."[17]

Finney was articulating a progressivist religiosity which
matched the sense of expansion and discovery running
rampant throughout the nation in the 1820s and 30s.
"New measures," he wrote, "are necessary from time to
time to awaken attention and to bring the gospel to bear
upon the public mind."[18] The only test of a religious belief
was whether it produced results. Not surprisingly, most of
the "new measures" developed by Finney and his cohorts
emphasized the human role in initiating the regenerative
process. According to Whitney Cross, the instrumental
role played by the revivalist established "the notion that
special efforts under a person of particular talents would
create a keener spirituality than the ordinary course of
events could achieve."[19]

What historians have labeled the "burned-over" phenomenon occuring within American culture between 1800
and 1850 testifies to the eccentricity of the religious innovations set in motion by the Second Great Awakening.
During this period religious fervor reached a stage of intensity which prompted many to compare the spread of
experiential forms of religion with the ravaging flames of
a forest fire. Termed "ultraism" by contemporaries, this
peculiarly American religious creation has been described

by Whitney Cross as a "combination of activities, personalities, and attitudes creating a condition of society which
could foster experimental doctrines." Mormonism, Shak-
erism, Adventism, communitarianism, and millenarian-
ism, all emerged among those engaged in a protracted
search for new ways of getting "the automatically operant
Holy Spirit to descend and symbolize the start of the New
Life."[20] Innovation was, as Cross notes, at the very heart
of the period's quest:

> Popular demand, whetted by constant revivals, invited
> ever-more-novel departures. Finney's relatively sane
> popularizing tendency grew among his emulators into
> a mania. More than one itinerant may have claimed to
> be "recipient and channel of a sensible divine emana-
> tion, which he caused to pass from him by a perceptible
> influence, as electricity passes from one body to anoth-
> er."[21]

That mesmerism entered into American cultural life as
but one more permutation of the nation's revivalist heritage is, then, not at all surprising. The mesmerists traveled
from town to town on a New England circuit nearly identical to that of the revivalists. Some came to hear about this
strange healing science out of sheer curiosity; but many
came out of sheer desperation. Those harboring doubts
about themselves or their ability to get a firmer grip on
life were naturally vulnerable to the mesmerists' impassioned rhetoric concerning the "true" secret to human fulfillment. And, like the revivalists before them, the
mesmerists preached that confusion, self-doubt, and de-
moralization would continue to plague people as long as
they refused to open themselves up to a higher spiritual
power.

Mesmerism, no less than revivalism, provided confused individuals with an intense experience thought to bring them into an interior harmony with unseen spiritual forces. It, too, gave convincing demonstration of the power of man's spiritual nature over the errant tendencies of his lower, animal nature. Yet the mesmerists differed in at least one respect. Instead of reproaching individuals for their tendency to impose human reason onto the ways of God, they actually encouraged it. John Dods elaborated at length on the fact that "man is intellectually a progressive being."

> As the Creator of the universe has endowed man with reason, and assigned him a noble and intelligent rank in the scale of intellectual and moral being—and as he has commanded him to use this faculty—so I may with justice remark, that he who cannot reason is a fool; he who dare not reason is a coward; he who will not reason, is a bigot.[22]

Those infected by the Arminian spirit found mesmerism a much welcomed substitute for the messy business of contrition and self-flagellation formerly thought indispensable to the process of regeneration. It was now possible to speak of the difference between man's higher and lower natures in nontheological language. The more intellectually sophisticated considered mesmerism to be opening a passage from the highest point of science into spiritual philosophy.[23] This early psychological doctrine thus played right into the hands of those wishing to carry their progressivist religious outlook to its furthest possible conclusions.

Mesmerism's gradual entry into nineteenth-century American religious life eludes straightforward explication.

Its adherents never organized into a denomination or fellowship. A popular psychology, mesmerism had no formal relationship with any one religious creed. Yet at the same time, its doctrinal neutrality made it a diffuse source of many of the period's most-innovative departures from mainstream Protestantism.

The only comprehensive assessment of American religious life written at the time of mesmerism's appearance was Robert Baird's *Religion in America.* Baird's account was a quite unapologetic critique of existing religious denominations written from the theological standpoint of evangelical Protestantism. In retrospect the book is more valuable for what it omitted than for its predictably jaundiced characterization of known friends and foes. Accustomed to thinking in terms of denominational affiliation, Baird was wholly oblivious to the religious import of an unchurched movement like mesmerism. But his description of current sectarian tendencies provides an invaluable clue as to why what Poyen had called a "science of man's mental and moral constitution" so readily became entangled in the major doctrinal controversies of the day. Baird observed that the proliferation of sectarian bodies could be traced to their varying interpretations as to how the mind comes under the influence of the Holy Spirit. Rival sects engaged in incessant "debates about the constitution of the mind, the analysis of responsibility and moral agency, and the age-old question of fate and free will."[24] From Baird's remark it would seem that the period's volatile religious discussions grew out of an intellectual dilemma rooted in the revialists' dual concern with personal experience and moral effort. New doctrines were constantly being advanced in the attempt to explain the "constitution of the mind" in such a way that man could be considered capable of being guided by the Holy Spirit while remaining an autonomous moral agent in his own right.

A pious church historian like Baird was methodologically blind to the nonecclesiastical sources which inform popular religiosity. Yet significant changes in the nature of American spirituality were taking shape right under Baird's eyes. The intense revival activity spawned by the Second Great Awakening had already subsided by the late 1830s. This is not to say that revivalism's experimental thrust thereafter disappeared, but that it drifted even further beyond the confines of denominational affiliation. During the 40s and 50s many former revivalists transferred their fervor to what they considered more progressive religious causes. In particular, spiritualism, Universalism, and Swedenborgianism, all drew from the ranks of those seeking to sustain their earlier religious enthusiasms through ever more daring departures from the mainstream tradition. All three of these groups responded to a growing concern to unite the forms of both ecstatic experience and "scientific" thinking in a single religious system. Unfortunately, they were able to find precious little scriptural warrant for their theological innovations. Having stepped outside Christian orthodoxy, they now faced the problem of legitimating their newly minted beliefs and practices.

Many of those wishing to circumvent lifeless theological doctrines in their effort to rediscover the essence of religion were emboldened by the mesmerists' discoveries. It is important to recall that, in the 1840s, the war between science and religion hadn't yet been declared. Under the influence of Scottish realism, especially in its Lockean rendering, sensory experience was considered to be the foundation of all human knowledge—even in the religious sphere. Unsullied confidence in the predetermined harmony of the universe permitted religious thinkers to view science as containing compelling evidence of God's existence and perfection. Even Protestant clergymen considered scientific descriptions of nature second only to Scripture as a source of information about God.[25] Whitney Cross has aptly summarized popular expectations concerning new scientific discoveries:

> Before they ever heard of Mesmer or Swedenborg, they expected new scientific discoveries to confirm the broad patterns of revelation as they understood them: to give mankind ever-more-revealing glimpses of the preordained divine plan for humanity and the universe. They expected all such knowledge would demonstrate the superiority of ideal over physical or material force, and that it would prove the relationship of man's soul to the infinite spiritual power.[26]

The reason for the quick appropriation of mesmerism by fringe religious groups was that mesmerism went all other sciences of the period one better. It showed how human experience extended well beyond the boundaries of the physical senses. Mesmerized subjects proved that sensory experience was not the only, nor even the highest, form of mental "impressibility." As Grimes put it, mesmerism had once and for all exposed "the deficiency of Locke's system in relation to the spontaneous operations of the mind independently of external sensations."[27] Mystical illumination and ecstatic revelation needed no longer to be dismissed as fanciful irrationalities. They, too, were under the jurisdiction of a suitably enlarged science of the mind and its powers. Léger commended mesmerism to fellow Christians of a liberal persuasion because it "not only disposes the mind to adopt religious principles, but also tends to free us from the errors of superstition by reducing to natural causes many phenomena."[28]

The mesmerists' hierarchical model of consciousness bore directly upon what Baird referred to as debates concerning "the constitution of the mind." For example, Buchanan followed the mesmerists' discoveries along a path leading from medical physiology to spiritualism. A former Methodist minister and sometime abolitionist, Sunderland also thought that mesmerism's investigations of the unconscious mind led to a spiritualist conclusion. William Fishbough argued that mesmerism forged the connecting link between a Universalist ministry and his later absorption in spiritualist theology. John Dods also spent several years in a Universalist pulpit before deciding that electrical psychology was a more relevant framework within which to describe man's spiritual potentials. And George Bush was attracted to mesmerism when he discovered that it lent scientific backing to his Swedenborgian convictions.

Nor was it happenstance that Universalists, Swedenborgians, and spiritualists found mesmerism a reassuring ally. All three of these newcomers to the American religious scene refused to identify spirituality with moral conduct and personal piety. Theirs was what William Clebsch has described as an "esthetic spirituality." Esthetic spirituality here connotes "not so much the appreciation of beauty attributed to or inhering in objects of artistic creation but rather a consciousness of the beauty of living in harmony with divine things—in a word, being at home in the universe."[29] Clebsch makes a strong case that a clearly identifiable strain of esthetic religiosity has been in existence throughout the course of American history. Moreover, he believes that it can be considered the distinctive manner in which the American spirit relates to nature, to society, and to deity. This esthetic spirituality is expressed most eloquently in the writings of Jonathan Edwards, Ralph Waldo Emerson, and William James. All three emerged as eponymal figures in American religious life by exhorting their contemporaries to become inwardly receptive to the influx of spiritual energies. Over the years their writings have encouraged thousands to adopt a religious posture in which true spirituality is identified as an attitude wherein every event in nature is seen to be an expression of an immanent divinity.

As evidenced by mesmerism's course through the American popular mind, esthetic spirituality has had its lowbrow expressions, too; though they were proffered with considerably less intellectual persuasion than that provided by the pens of an Edwards or a James. The esthetic appreciation of man's inner-spirituality pervaded the religious thinking of Universalism, Swedenborgianism, and early spiritualism. It prompted them, even as it had the likes of Edwards and Emerson, to connect doctrines of theological immanence with some prerational dimension of human personality. This was not, strictly speaking, a pantheism. Their mission wasn't to repudiate the theological category of a First Cause. They merely insisted that all theological reflection should begin by focusing upon the point of contact between the divine and human spheres. And whatever the many differences among these religious movements, all three had their greatest appeal to those wishing to find this point of contact and in so doing to find themselves "at home in the universe."

The life and writings of John Dods provide a perfect example of how mesmerism assisted many nineteenth-century Americans in their effort to stake out and defend new territories of religious self-understanding. Dods's theological meanderings began with a brief stint as pastor of the Universalist Society Church in Provincetown, Massachusetts. The Universalists' insistence that all, not just a select few, will participate in eternal life put them at distinct odds with antebellum American Protestantism. In a volume entitled *Thirty Short Sermons, Both Doctrinal and Practical,* Dods charged orthodox doctrines about God and salvation with failing to meet the religious needs of his contemporaries.[30] The Calvinist God was one of "endless vengeance and woe"; conventional theology played upon persons' fears rather than filling their hearts with joy, serenity, and self-confidence. The true essence of Christianity, he asserted, was the experience of a New Birth through which earlier anxieties are replaced by unremitting exuberance. Being born again was in no sense a symbolic process as far as Dods was concerned. It was a very real, almost tangible, event in an individual's life. Spiritual rebirth consisted of gradually elevating the mind above the physical plane so as to experience "the spiritual body as a reality so that we may now live the regenerated joyful life."[31]

Where Dods differed from the many revivalist preachers also holding out religious conversion as the cure for maladies of the body and soul was that he refused to view the experience of spiritual rebirth as an all-or-nothing event. True religious growth, like other natural processes, evolves through distinct developmental stages. Dods preached that just as "natural birth presupposes the perfect formation of the body by that secret energy of nature only God can comprehend . . . [so the] second birth cannot take place until after the preparation of the spiritual body."[32] Dods wasn't quite sure as to the exact mechanism through which this "secret energy of nature" enters the mind. Nor, for that matter, could he pinpoint the physiological process whereby this energy regenerates the physical and emotional systems. He could only conjecture that spirit must enter in through some mysterious "connexion between the mind and the body so subtle that it had hitherto eluded the eagle eye of physiology, and will perhaps remain inscrutable forever to human comprehension."[33]

As it turned out, this connection was not nearly so inscrutable. Just a few years later Dods came across the very principle interconnecting the human and spiritual realms—animal magnetism. The discovery of the mesmeric state of consciousness put his previous conjectures about the New Birth on solid intellectual ground. Beset by the same penchant for one-ideaism found in other religious radicals of the age, Dods hit upon mesmerism as the single panacea for most every human ill.[34] He promptly left the ministry and devoted the rest of his life to the study and dissemination of "electrical psychology." According to Dods, a science of man's psychological constitution opened new avenues for understanding life's inner-spirituality. It could now be confidently asserted that, through our possession of animal magnetism, every last one of us is in direct contact with "the grand agent employed by the Creator to move and govern the universe."[35] Dods fairly enticed his readers to consider "how sublime the idea that God is electrically and magnetically connected with His universe, that this is how He stamps upon the world its BEAUTY, ORDER, and HARMONY, which are but reflected impressions of His own splendor."[36] Insofar as God is magnetically connected with the universe, the mesmerizing process was something of a sacrament. Dods was convinced that, when properly employed, it had the power to "enlarge and elevate the mind . . . to impress upon it more-exalted ideas of the Deity."[37]

It occurred to Dods that mesmerism provided the theoretical framework for a new, psychologically formulated *imago dei*. God is spirit; and man, through his possession of animal magnetism, is himself a "visible daguerreotype" of God's electrical emanations.[38] And just as the human mind has both a cerebrum, which contains man's voluntary mental powers, and a cerebellum, which executes his involuntary mental powers, so can Divine Mind be said to consist of both voluntary and involuntary spiritual powers. God's voluntary powers become evident during those rare instances in which He miraculously interferes with the laws of nature. God's involuntary activities are executed through the invariant laws of nature as set down at the time of creation. The "unchanging laws of the universe are but the unchanging thoughts of God."[39] Hence man, through the medium of animal magnetism, has continual recourse to the guiding wisdom of Divine Mind.

With the help of mesmerist psychology, Dods had dealt a final blow to the fickle God of Calvinism. No longer a remote, inscrutable judge of human actions, God was now understood to be an impersonal power in nature. Nor did mesmerist psychology stop at merely accumulating evidence of God's presence in nature as did other scientific theories. It took the further step of explicitly reassuring individuals that they could and should trust their inner promptings. The powers of human reason are at root divine. In Dods's view, mesmerism had furnished "positive proof that man has instinct and intuition in the back of his brain . . . it is through these that God inspires man."[40]

Dods's sustained effort to envision man as a psychosomatic unity was one of the earliest installments in what persists to this day as an identifiable tradition in popular American religious thought. Long before Mary Baker Eddy, Norman Vincent Peale, Scientology, or Transcendental Meditation, Dods employed contemporary psychological ideas for the purpose of identifying physical vigor with religiousness. Dods thought it a psychological fact that "there is but one grand cause of disease: which is the electricity of the system thrown out of balance."[41] From this postulate it was possible to deduce various attitudinal traits which cause individuals to fall prey to their own misdirected energies: restlessness, complacency, fault finding, fear, and above all, chronic dissatisfaction with the events of Providence. Dods was also quick to add "shutting up, repressing our mental woes," to his list of self-defeating tendencies.[42]

Sin is not a matter of disbelief but rather a psychological condition in which the mind comes under the dominance of external conditions. Man, insofar as he is created in the image of God, stands rightfully at the head of the created universe. Dods understood this to mean that the mind is so constituted that we ought to strive to be receptive toward all that is above us on the cosmological scale, and active toward all that is below. The mesmeric state of consciousness revealed that we all have access to mental states

that of lending "scientific" plausibility to the religious visions of the movement's founder. An eminent scientist in his day, Emanuel Swedenborg (1688–1771) had already made significant contributions in such varied fields as physics, astronomy, and anatomy before finally dedicating himself to the study of the secret mysteries contained in Christian Scripture. To state that his ideas were unorthodox would be to put the matter mildly. Swedenborg claimed that, while in states of mystical reverie, he had been granted "perfect inspiration." Fortunately for those of us not quite so gifted at receiving verbal dispensation, Swedenborg was not nearly as reticent as mystical seers are usually wont to be. In all he wrote more than thirty volumes purporting to uncover the hidden spiritual meanings buried beneath the literal sense of Christian doctines.

Swedenborg's writings appealed to those wishing to break with church tradition. His revelations freed the essence of the Christian message from bondage to ancient events. Swedenborg was himself living proof that the truths of religion could be known directly through inward illumination. He explained that the universe is composed of several interpenetrating dimensions—physical, mental, spiritual, angelic, etc. Each of these dimensions is in some invisible way connected with every other. It followed that complete harmony in any one dimension of life depends upon establishing rapport with other levels on the cosmic scale. All true progress proceeds according to influences received from above. The physical body achieves inner harmony by first becoming attuned with the soul, the soul through contact with superior angelic beings, and so on up the spiritual ladder. Through diligent study and prolonged introspection, anyone might obtain the requisite gnosis to make contact with higher spiritual planes. The benefits to be obtained were thought to be numerous: spontaneous insight into cosmological secrets; conversations with angelic beings; intuitive understanding of scriptural verses; and the instantaneous healing of both physical and emotional disorders.

Swedenborg's undaunted confidence in the soul's capacity for limitless development contrasted sharply with the Calvinists' insistence upon human depravity. His wondrous doctrines found wide circulation among the many sectarian groups which populated the nineteenth-century religious landscape.[49] Communitarians, Transcendentalists, faith healers, spiritualists, and wealthy dilettantes were alike encouraged by his expansive doctrines. John Humphrey Noyes understood well the reasons for the movement's appeal to diverse religious and intellectual dispositions:

> The Bible and revivals had made men hungry for something more than social reconstruction. Swedenborg's offer of a new heaven as well as a new earth, met the demand magnificently. . . . The scientific were charmed, because he was primarily a man of science, and seemed to reduce the world to scientific order. The mystics were charmed because he led them boldly into all the mysteries of intuition and invisible worlds.[50]

Swedenborg, via his multifaceted doctrine of correspondence, held that men and women are inwardly constructed so as to be able to receive "psychic influx" from higher planes of reality. But since saying so didn't necessarily make it so, many of his disciples struggled to articulate the physiological details. Thus it was that Swedenborg's American followers gave scrupulous attention to every word of his essay "On the Intercourse Between the Soul and the Body Which is Supposed to Take Place Either by Physical Influx or by Pre-Established Harmony." Most seemed to favor the idea of physical influx. For example, Emerson concluded that the mind is "an organ recipient of life from God."[51] Similarly an 1838 edition of the movement's principal voicepiece, the *New Jerusalem Magazine*, clumsily suggested that "life from God flows-in into man through the soul, and through this into the mind, that is, into the reflections and thoughts of the mind, and from these into the sense, speech and actions of the body."[52]

Small wonder that Robert Baird was dumbfounded by Swedenborgianism's presence on the American religious scene. Baird denounced its doctrines as a strange amalgamation of heresies including "some of the most extravagant vagaries of mysticism." He warned that it "unsettles the mind and leaves it prey to the wildest whimsies that it is possible for the human mind to create or entertain."[53] Baird never relaxed his theological guard long enough to appreciate the sincerity of the Swedenborgians' efforts to bring new life to Christian doctrines. It never dawned upon him that they, too, were engaged in debates about the constitution of the mind and its susceptibility to spiritual influences. The only nonpejorative comment Baird was able to make about the movement was that it had stirred the passions of religious liberals. He noted that "in some cases men who have grown tired of the coldness of Unitarians have betaken themselves to Swedenborgianism. Dr. Bush is their ablest writer."[54]

It is to Dr. Bush, then, to whom we will look in order to link mesmerism with this most ubiquitous of the period's theological innovations. In 1847 Bush published a scholarly defense of his beliefs on the grounds that they had been fully confirmed by recent scientific discoveries. The very title, *Mesmer and Swedenborg,* made his intentions clear and unmistakable. Bush took it for granted that his readers already acknowledged mesmerism's scientific credentials. Any association between the Swedish seer and the wizard from Vienna would be to benefit the former. And for good reason; it was by this time quite clear that "the undubitable facts of mesmerism are affording to the many senses of man a demonstration which cannot be resisted, that Swedenborg has told the truth of the other life."[55]

Bush claimed to have thoroughly studied most of the two thousand works already published on the subject of animal magnetism. He concluded that "when taken together, the investigations of the mesmeric state point to an entirely new class of facts in psychology." And, more to the point, this new class of facts buttressed the Swedenborgian system by proving "the grand principle that man is a spirit as to his interiors and that his spiritual nature in the body often manifests itself according to the laws which govern it out of the body."[56] It almost seemed to Bush that mesmerism had "been developed in this use with the express design of confirming the message of Swedenborg."

The reports of entranced subjects could be safely considered descriptions of a higher plane of consciousness. Bush himself experimented with mesmerism and found clear evidence of the existence of extrasensory perception, telepathy, and clairvoyance. Many of his subjects reported having had periods of mystical rapture as they came under the influence of this numinous state of consciousness.

93

Some even told of having seen "mental atmospheres" composed of ultrafine rays of light surrounding persons' heads. Surely animal magnetism must be the medium of psychic influx postulated by Swedenborgian metaphysics all along.

Mesmerist psychology offered Bush and other Swedenborgians a scientific analysis of the mind "just at that point where anthropology welds itself to Theology."[57] Its experiments clearly established the existence of higher spiritual levels. Mesmerized subjects offered brilliant testimonials verifying the kinds of claims for which Swedenborgians had long been ridiculed. "They speak as if, to their own consciousness, they had undergone an inward translation by which they had passed out of a material into a spiritual body. . . . The state into which a subject is brought by the mesmerizing process is a state in which the spirit predominates for the time being over the body."[58] Swedenborgians wishing to communicate to nonbelievers from an apologetic standpoint were now in possession of a persuasive hermeneutic. Bush was fully cognizant of how this independent corroboration might strengthen the Swedenborgian cause in America. "On the whole it must, we think, be admitted that the phenomena of mesmerism taken in conjunction with the developments of Swedenborg, open a new chapter in the philosophy of mind and in man's relations to a higher sphere."[59] The discovery of the mesmeric state of consciousness was, thus, of timely importance to the movement's attempt to bring Americans into a "new view of the interior genius of the inspired word, and of the whole body of Christian doctrine."[60] Not even a Charles Finney would have dreamed of a more savvy proselytizing device.

94

The psychological doctrines which framed a natural sacrament for certain Universalists and the means of psychic influx for Swedenborgians were, in yet another metaphysical setting, transposed into a technology for communicating with departed relatives. Nineteenth-century spiritualism comprised such a diverse array of beliefs and practices that almost any set of generalizations can be faulted for oversimplification. The term *spiritualism* usually refers to a concoction of quasi-religious activities which are, if not historically, at least cosmetically linked to the table rapping phenomena which occurred at the Hydesville, New York, home of the Fox sisters. Fraudulent or not, the Fox sisters' séances rallied public support for a movement which, by the 1870s, could claim as many as eleven million believers.

The gaudy séances and obvious deceptions for which the spiritualist movement is best known have the unfortunate consequence of obscuring the esthetic spirituality which permeated its earliest phases. In his study of the historical development of spiritualism, R. Laurence Moore makes a helpful distinction between those spiritualists seeking mystical illumination and those out to master the craft of mediumship. The medium, he writes, "receives unreliable information from nondivine sources and undergoes no inward transformation as a result of the experience."[61] While the distinction is at best a hazy one, it does draw attention to a very real shift in the dominant tone of American spiritualism; a shift which, it should be noted, progressively emphasized mediumistic extravaganzas at the expense of concern for inner-sanctification.

Thomas Lake Harris and Andrew Jackson Davis typify those who viewed the trance state as an avenue through which to discover one's own true divinity. Harris, yet another Universalist minister, equated religious faith with a living sense of "the Divinity within." True theological convictions were experiential, not intellectual. He wrote that "to believe in God is but to believe that the spirit which we feel flowing into ourselves flows from an Infinite Existing Source."[62] Of course, the kind of religiosity Harris had in mind has a fairly stiff prerequisite attached—a prior belief that humans can, and regularly do, feel spirit flowing into themselves. And this is exactly what he considered spiritualism to be all about. What he described as the spiritualist state of consciousness was one which consecrated the senses. Spiritualism was essentially sacramental in character in that it allowed the world in its every part to be seen as teeming with divine beauty. Harris's esthetic sensibility caused him to join both Davis and LaRoy Sunderland in denouncing spiritualism's later preoccupation with outer manifestations. He feared that such activities invariably direct attention away from the "spirit of Christ, which descends to be immanent in the heart."[63]

Andrew Jackson Davis's story merits closer attention. The details of his life are questionable to say the least, since most must be garnered from his autobiographical reflections.[64] No real matter. If Davis rearranged or even fabricated a few events here and there, so much the better. The fact that he later attributed such dramatic importance to his quest for religious certainty is itself a datum of historical importance; for, to hear Davis tell it, his was the most wretched existence imaginable until mesmerism healed him of his doubts and put him in touch with an altogether new source of religious authority.

Davis recounts his life as though it were one long, religious, obstacle course. The various denominations thwarted him at every step of the way. As a youth Davis regularly attended Presbyterian catechism where he was taught of a "God clothed in Calvinist attributes, also in His eternal decrees of election and reprobation and also in many other points of faith ascribing unamiable qualities to the Deity."[65] Whether out of persistence or petulance—or both, Davis took it upon himself to cross-examine his teachers as to how all of this could be so. His queries met only with admonishments that it must be a very depraved and hell-bent boy who would dare reason into the ways of God. When Calvinism proved to be too restrictive for his inquisitive mind, he set out in search of a more hospitable denomination. Unfortunately, he fared no better with the Methodists. Their "program for prayer and conversion" failed to satisfy his craving for total certainty. It soon became apparent that no ready-made religious doctrine, no matter how liberal its cast, could contain Davis's spiritual wanderlust. He relates that "by another year I was introduced to Universalism. Its teachings were more congenial with my better nature . . . [but] I couldn't believe the Universalist system of theology as a whole."[66]

It was a peculiar quirk of fate that rescued Davis from a life of spiritual impoverishment. In 1843 a mesmerist by the name of J. Stanley Grimes passed through his hometown of Poughkeepsie giving lecture-demonstrations on the subject of animal magnetism. Grimes's astonishing displays prompted a local townsman to do some experimenting on his own. He randomly selected the young Davis for a subject. Davis, who was at the time an appren-

97

tice cobbler, quickly developed remarkable skill as a trance performer. In no time at all he was reading from books while blindfolded, reporting of clairvoyant travels to distant locales, and duplicating other well-known mesmeric feats. He hired himself out as a professional trance subject and for a time toured New England, exhibiting his miraculous mental powers. After several months of repeated journeys into the inner recesses of his mind, Davis up and declared that mesmerism had activated "some of the many powers which we know to rest in the soul's deep bosom."[67] The greatest of these powers was the ability to channel wisdom down from out of the spiritual ethers in the form of verbal messages. Mesmerism had unwittingly played midwife to trance mediumship.

Davis soon learned to dispense with outside assistance and enter a self-induced mesmeric trance. While in this special mental state, "mighty and sacred truths spontaneously gushed up from the depths of my spirit."[68] By now all of this had become rather perfunctory; however, Davis insisted that these truths were communicated to him by departed spirits. From the vantage point of heaven, Davis's contacts had valuable lessons to teach. For the most part they confined themselves to subjects intended to assist men and women with their spiritual advancement. Friends feverishly recorded every word so that they might later be published. The American public fairly gobbled up these dispensations. Davis's major work, *The Harmonial Philosophy,* went through twenty-four editions.

For all their vacuity, the materials written "by and through" Andrew Jackson Davis espoused an eminently respectable religiosity. His spirit messages contained moral exhortations and remonstrances concerning the spiritual importance of inwardly centering oneself in the universe. Perhaps Davis courted a higher class of discarnate friends than his colleagues, for he rarely channeled the banal reassurances from departed loved ones which later jammed the psychic airwaves. His "harmonial philosophy" taught that one grand set of divinely appointed principles ruled the universe in its every expression. Those who learned to develop their spiritual sense in congruence with their physical ones would immediately inhabit a world admitting of no discordance.

If all of this sounds a bit like Swedenborg, well, in a manner of speaking it was. Or, at least, so Davis's contact on the other side occasionally identified himself. George Bush was so thoroughly convinced that Davis had struck correspondence with the spirit of the Swedish seer that he included a short appendix entitled "The Revelation of Andrew Jackson Davis" in his *Mesmer and Swedenborg.* Bush notes with astonishment that, from the mesmeric state, this poorly educated cobbler spoke fluent Greek, Hebrew, Latin, and Sanskrit. Surely Davis was too much of a dimwit to pull off such an elaborate ruse. Nor could he possibly have access to all the scientific information contained in his philosophy.[69] Bush didn't think himself competent to express an opinion as to the scientific merit of Davis's metaphysics. He was, however, prepared to testify to "the fact of his making correct use of a multitude of technical terms appropriate to the themes of science, which he is wholly unable to define in his waking state and which . . . he utilizes with entire freedom and corrections in the mesmeric delivery."[70] The medium was apparently more interesting than his message.

The further spiritualism drifted toward mediumistic activity, the less likely it was to find mesmerism fit company. Trance mediums receive verbal communications from dead persons, not magnetic fluids. Psychological theories were of little or no use when it came to substantiating spirit messages. Spiritualists grew ever more insistent that their activities could be scientifically demonstrated under conditions that minimized subjective mental influences. They slavishly imitated scientific method to the point of shunning subjectivity and inwardness as things which really didn't count.[71] The spiritualists' ability to attract a paying clientele depended more on reassuring them as to their dead relatives' well-being than convincing them of their own inner-spirituality.

The apotheosis of mesmerism from a psychological doctrine to a source of popular religiosity owed much to the existence of scattered groups of persons willing to experiment with new and progressivist understandings of man's relationship to God.[72] Whitney Cross has remarked of the period that in many cases "mesmerism led to Swedenborgianism, and Swedenborgianism to spiritualism, not because of the degree of intrinsic relationship between their propositions but because of the assumptions according to which their American adherents understood them."[73] These assumptions were precisely those put into popular currency with the intensification of revival campaigns. It was sheer happenstance that mesmerism arrived in the United States amidst the tumultuous aftermath of the awakening that loosened American religious thought from a strictly Calvinist outlook to one more in keeping with an age of progress and expansion. The science of animal magnetism was swept along in the wake of what William McLoughlin aptly describes as a folk movement through which "a people or a nation reshapes its identity, transforms its patterns of thought and action, and sustains a healthy relationship with environmental and social change."[74] Thus when Americans turned to these early psychological doctrines, it was most definitely not for the purpose of eradicating cultural norms. To the contrary. The mesmerists' doctrines, like other innovations brought about by the Second Great Awakening, were advanced by those seeking new ways "to maintain faith in ourselves, our ideals, and our covenant with God even while they compel us to reinterpret that covenant in light of new experience."[75]

Descriptions of latent psychological potentials redefined the details but kept the covenantal bond between the divine and human spheres fully intact. Those willing to be persuaded by the mesmerists' claim that a continuum or orderly hierarchy exists between the lower and higher reaches of human nature found psychology a natural derivative of covenantal conceptions of man's religious responsibilities. Psychological ideas were, so to speak, the lowest common denominator to which they could reduce otherwise hopelessly abstract considerations concerning how to align themselves with the greater scheme of things. This new slant on human nature "at just that point where anthropology welds itself to theology" was particularly appealing to those yearning to feel directly related to God yet cringing at the thought of joining an established church or subscribing to dead theological formulations.

In all of this the nation's first psychological system retained important continuities with the fundamental tenets of the Puritan-Protestant world view. That is, it reaffirmed faith in the predetermined harmony of all natural and historical processes; the belief that inner-adjustment (faith) is prior to good works; and the essentially religious character of the individual's struggle to seek out and ascetically order his life in conformity with the ultimate conditions of reality. Though mesmerism introduced novel terms about Americans' self-interpretation, it still affirmed what McLoughlin calls the "congeries of conceptions" at the core of American culture:

> the chosen nation; the convenant with God; the millenial manifest destiny; the higher (biblical or natural) law . . .; the laws of science, presumed to be from the Creator, and evolutionary or progressive in their purpose; the work ethic (or "Protestant ethic"), which holds that equal opportunity and hard work will bring economic success and public respect to all who assert and discipline themselves; and the benevolence of nature under the exploitive or controlling hand of man (i.e., nature was made for man).[76]

To this extent nineteenth-century Americans were able to view mesmerism and Christian faith as not only compatible but actually implicative of one another. Joseph Haddock echoed an important undercurrent in the mesmerists' literature when he carefully marshaled evidence to show that "the philosophy of Christianity appears to offer the easiest and most rational solution of the higher mesmeric phenomena, especially as regards the state of exstasis or trance."[77] He further concluded "that the narrative of the New Testament and the facts of mesmerism are mutually explanatory and corroborative of each other." Americans' interest in mesmerism reflected the gradual shift in American religious conviction away from sole dependence upon biblical passages over to what might be called "religious anthropology."[78] If one were to compare the theologies of, say, Lyman Beecher and Nathaniel Taylor to those of Henry Ward Beecher and Horace Bushnell, it would seem that mesmerism was at the forefront of the same liberalizing tendencies that were destined to appear eventually in the mainstream denominations if they were to keep apace of changing sociocultural realities.

Mesmerism's successful entry into American intellectual life was, in the last analysis, due to its ability to locate new experiential moorings for a progressive spirituality. Psychological theories transposed the form of personal piety from categories of theological transcendence to those of "natural law" and thus accommodated the conceptual needs of an age enticed by the promise of science and technology. Psychological principles had the further advantage of recasting the forces upon which human nature is dependent onto the more comfortable vernacular of scientific laws of cause and effect. A miracle, Dods wrote, "is nothing more than the operation of mind in direct communication with this creative energy [animal magnetism]."[79] Townshend stated that mesmerism had not only shown that miracles are but the activation of faculties inherent in man, but that it had also proved the faculties "to be improvable and capable of development, the limits of which have not been ascertained."[80] Mesmerism thus made it possible for at least some Americans to believe that they had gained a measure of control over what was previously the most capricious area of their lives.

The Americanization of animal magnetism finally drove psychology clear out of its mind. Psychological reasoning had emerged in an age in which Americans were beginning to hunger for nonscriptural sources of spiritual edification. The American mesmerists responded by offering them an entirely new, and eminently attractive, arena for self-discovery—their own psychological depths. Their theories concerning psychological self-adjustment were carefully formulated so that they could be interpreted as the ontological equivalent of reconciling oneself with an immanent divinity. Mesmerism was, then, but the first in a long line of psychological systems that have attracted popular following precisely due to the fact that large segments of the American public yearn to reduce the sphere of their metaphysical responsibilities to more-manageable proportions. By the 1850s mesmerism had entered into the common stock of ideas from which many took their religious bearings on life. Its theories and methods promised to restore individuals, even unchurched ones, into harmony with the cosmic scheme. In a word, psychology had taken its first step toward constituting itself as an independent source for the religious cure of souls.

emotional needs, entered a decisively new phase in their contribution to the cure of American souls.[1]

The thirty years immediately following the Civil War saw almost every urban center in the Northeast triple in size. They were no longer large towns but massive metropolitan complexes. This transition from landscape to cityscape thrust American culture onto untested ground. And to add to the confusion, most of the more than forty million immigrants who arrived on the nation's shores in the latter half of the century headed straight for the city. As early as 1860 a full 37 percent of all city dwellers possessed languages, customs, and idiosyncrasies different from their Yankee "hosts." Suspicious of each other, immigrant groups retreated into self-imposed isolation. The United States was no longer the melting pot of world cultures, but rather a grab bag of divergent peoples.

Slums, crime, political conflict, and a myriad of other complications cluttered the American cityscape. Social blight served as a constant reminder that the nation was no longer a land of kindred spirits working toward common goals. The loss of social homogeneity proved to have a profound impact on the country's self-interpretation. Those Americans belonging to the pace-setting cultural mainstream were, for the first time, required to confront "the other." For better or worse, white, Anglo-Saxon Protestants and their way of life were being displaced from the center of the national experience, and many began to point fingers at those they held responsible. A Methodist minister in New York singled out a few of the culprits by compiling a long list of "forces opposed to the extension of Protestantism." He warned that urban crowding, saloons, Romanism, and a foreign element which refused to be assimilated were slowly chipping away at the nation's moral and spiritual leadership.[2] This list is, in retrospect, a kind of sociological epitaph of the Wasp hegemony over American cultural life. The increasingly plurastic character of American society now made "legislative, social, and religious problems difficult of solution."[3] In other words, older patterns were breaking down.

Prior to the 1870s, small-town life had been the country's norm. American communal life had been relatively cohesive, forged as it was around a pervasive consensus about the values of its predominantly Protestant, Anglo-Saxon populace. Human relationships were shaped within consensually validated norms and patterns. Americans took for granted

> every man's ability to know that God had ordained modesty in women, rectitude in men, thrift, sobriety, and hard work in both. People of very different backgrounds accommodated themselves to this Protestant code which had become so thoroughly identified with respectability. . . . In an island community people had little reason to believe that these daily precepts were not universally valid, and few doubted that the nation's ills were caused by men who dared to deny them.[4]

This "Protestant code" depended a great deal upon the economic and social sanctions wrought by the interdependence of small-town life. Voluntary cooperation, spontaneity, and gregariousness were not just virtues but practical necessities. In contrast, urban living generated its own special values which were destined to come into conflict with those of America's small-town heritage. Contractual agreement, systematic performance, and well-partitioned social roles undermined the moral orientation and social sense of those not reared in urban ways. Historian Robert Wiebe summarizes the impact of these changes with his comment that

> The health of the nineteenth-century community depended upon two closely related conditions: its ability to manage the lives of its members, and the belief among its members that the community had such powers. Already by the 1870's the autonomy of the community was badly eroded. . . . America in the late nineteenth century was a society without a core. It lacked those national centers of authority and information which might have given order to such swift changes.[5]

Cultural spokesmen, particularly those of the nation's churches, sought to arrest America's dissolution into a "society without a core." The solutions they advanced were generally pallid reaffirmations of traditional values. It proved far easier to give colorful descriptions of the flagrant problems besetting the country than to propose constructive measures for reform.

In an essay written in 1880, for example, John Spalding contrasted the decadence of urban living with the pristine simplicity of agrarian life.[6] He wrote that "every special mode of life creates a separate type of character, and the virtues and vices of races and nations are traceable in a great degree to the surroundings in which they have lived and labored." He went on to cite that rampant drunkenness, prostitution, and filth among the urban working class were proof that city life is incompatible with Christian ideals. His, like other essays and sermons of the period, clung to a rural nostalgia. It is the farmer who "is the strongest and healthiest member of the social body, he is also the most religious and most moral." In contrast, Spalding was hard pressed to find anything positive about city living. In fact, he deemed it to be downright parasitic. Urban dwellers seemed to lack the moral stamina of their rural counterparts. Spalding feared that urbanites were rapidly "spending the energies which their father's hard, silent life accumulated," and that they "will lack the energy to buffet the storm."

Like so many other denominational spokesmen of the period, Spalding came up with few concrete proposals for providing urban dwellers with more "energy." Church response to the early phases of American urbanization was unimaginative and often irrelevant. Those entrusted with the maintenance and dissemination of the cultural visions of the good society simply denied the city any permanent role in the shaping of America's destiny. Spalding, for instance, proposed uprooting the oppressed city dwellers and recolonizing them in the countryside. Cityscape was to be avoided if inherited patterns of religiosity were to remain intact.

The problems of industrialization went hand in hand with migration to the cities. The factory soon replaced the farm as the symbol of the nation's productivity, leaving wage earners utterly mystified. An agrarian economy provides individuals with a relatively simple vision of economic opportunity: success is a function of the expenditure of time and energy. An industrial order, however, doesn't permit such straightforward calculations. Few nineteenth-century Americans had the vision to see something objectively "out there" around which to set their sights and harness their energies. The obstacles standing in their way were no longer as tangible as rugged soil or broken fences. Who knew how to recognize a recession, cartels, or monopolies—much less overcome them? Americans lacked rules for reducing their complex world into manageable proportions. And without ready-made guides for action, many floundered.

Most nineteenth-century Americans had been nurtured in the philosophy of rugged individualism. Success was thought to be a simple function of conscientious effort. Diligence, sobriety, and earnestness had a way of serving both individual and community alike. But as commendable as these values might be in their proper setting, they couldn't be uncritically carried over into cityscape. A simple philosophy of individualism is a poor orientation to a world of stockmarkets, trusts, and invisible labor pools. There are too many mediating factors in an industrial economy to insure any correspondence between individual sincerity and social reward.

Unable to make sense of the correspondence between their private and public lives, Americans were confused about which of the two required adjustment. Those ascribing to the Protestant ethic, not knowing how or where to channel their incessant anxieties, experienced an understandable frustration. Industrial society was too complex for methodical inner-direction. The new socioeconomic order understandably led to the demise of the Protestant work ethic. Individuals were no longer able to directly control their own material destinies. A major consequence was, according to Sydney Ahlstrom, that "individualism in the old sense became a liability for all but the industrial and banking tycoons."[7] The gulf between the private and public spheres was for many impassable. Motivation and inner desire naturally waned in those who felt permanently cut off from access to life's resources.

All the while American society was dividing into three main groups: (1) the definitely victorious, who were regarded as cultural heroes or true, representative men; (2) the definitely defeated, who were without hope of rising above the urban slum; and (3) the middle group, who were ceaselessly striving to make their way to the top. This final group included America's large middle class that was attempting to exert just that extra bit of effort to insure their upward climb. It is they who were most susceptible to, and would in fact create a market for, popular psychologies capable of organizing their energies into productive channels.

It would be no exaggeration to say that the "glue" which had previously bonded American society together had either evaporated or simply decomposed. Without some democratic principle with which to interpret the means for fulfilling individual destiny, Americans were pitted only against one another in their scramble to participate in the providential surge of God's created order. Churchman Washington Gladden lamented that American society had splintered into "scattered, diverse, alienated, antipathetic groups." Gladden was sensitive to the fact that intensified conflict over economic resources had eroded the very basis of community feeling.

> It is not very many years since society in this country was quite homogeneous; the economical distinction between capitalist and laborer was not clearly marked. . . . But our national process has given full scope to the principle of differentiation. . . . Anyone can see that progress, under a system like ours, must tend to the separation of men, and to the creation of a great many diverse and apparently unrelated elements. Under this

process men tend to become unsympathetic, jealous, antagonistic; the social bond is weakened.[8]

American culture was losing its organicity. What Gladden called the "centrifugal motion" of modern life intensified awareness of the differences rather than the similarities between persons. Social roles and status came to reflect little more than the separation of individuals into groups possessing more and less. Warmth and immediacy in human relationships gave way to contractual role expectations. The public sphere of life operated according to impersonal rules which did little to kindle a cohesive cultural bond. Few Americans believed theirs to be a society built upon what Victor Turner calls communitas. That is, the "essential and genuine human bond, without which there could be no society" was temporarily at low ebb.[9] Corporate life lacked an *élan vital,* or animating sense of humankindness. As a consequence, growing numbers of Americans found themselves confused, bewildered, and beleaguered—without access to the resources which would make them and their world whole and of a piece.

Rampant culture dis-ease took its toll on the stability of personal life. Dr. George Beard, a New York neurologist of the 1870s and 80s, gave succinct definition to what many had already begun to fear.[10] American character was beset with "nervous exhaustion." The symptoms were many: hysteria, headaches, insomnia, inebriety, cerebral irritation, premature baldness, hopelessness, fear of being alone, fear of society, fear of fears. Beard discounted theories attributing neurasthenic ailments to characterological imbalances or organic disorders. American nervousness was strictly a deficiency or lack of nerve force; it was a condition of nervous bankruptcy.

Beard had no trouble locating the root cause of American nervousness. Modern civilization was robbing its citizens of all their mental energy. No other period in world history had ever required so many mental tasks as did American modernity. Railway travel, the periodical press, the telegraph, religious liberties, the mental activity of women, Protestantisms and religious excitement generally, loud noises, the specialization of labor, social conventions that suppress emotional expression, and the chaotic flux of new ideas were all sapping individuals of their mental strength. The human brain just wasn't equipped to handle so many functions. Beard found that urban dwellers and those in brain-working families in the eastern portions of the United States were suffering the most. He reasoned that the lifestyle demanded of "civilized, refined, and educated" persons rendered them tragically susceptible to this psychological impotency.

Beard illustrated the consequences of nervous exhaustion with an analogy to Edison's recently discovered electric light. The human nervous system, like an electrical circuit, can adequately support only a limited number of operations.

> [When] new functions are interposed in the circuit, as modern civilization is constantly requiring us to do, there comes a period, sooner or later, varying in different individuals, and at different times of life, when the amount of force is insufficient to keep all the lamps burning; those that are weakest go out entirely, or as more frequently happens, burn faint and feebly—they do not expire; but give an insufficient and unstable light—this is the philosophy of modern nervousness.[11]

"Insufficient and unstable light" translated to psychosomatic illness. And, as Beard observed, this was an ever more frequently recurring phenomenon. The prognosis for American character disorders wasn't good at all. Beard predicted that there would be an increasing incidence of nervous exhaustion for at least the next quarter century. Modern civilization was not likely to stop advancing, and the human brain just wouldn't be up to the task. Any substantial improvements would have to await the evolutionary development of sturdier neural equipment. In the meantime his contemporaries would just have to learn to cope with faint and feebly glowing minds.

Beard's diagnosis implicitly indicted American culture with inefficiently channeling the human energies at its disposal. The high incidence of American nervousness attested to the rigorous demands which a pluralistic society places upon systematic inner-direction. Individuals were constantly being forced back upon their own resources. Confronted with difficult choices in nearly every area of their lives, many at last fell prey to their own indecisiveness. Their illnesses testified to an agonizing paradox: afflictor and afflicted were one and the same. Outer symptoms mirrored inner conflict. Worse yet, there appeared no way out of the syndrome of nervous exhaustion. Diligence and redoubled effort could only overtax, not replenish, precious human energies. The debilitated individual by definition lacked the inner resources to bring about a full recovery. Help would have to come from without. But where were these extrapersonal energies to be found? Who would point the way?

Sadly, the churches were of little help. Intellectual secularism and social pluralism combined to undermine the single most effective ritual at their disposal—revivalism. Revivalism had flourished in what was a comparatively unsophisticated social and intellectual environment. Inner-renewal from contact with the Holy Spirit was thought to lead automatically to one or another version of Calvinist piety. The revivalists had enjoyed the luxury of concentrating on the motivational element in spiritual living, knowing full well that the church community possessed sanctions for enjoining born-again persons to responsible moral conduct. But, by the 1860s, Protestant churches lacked the social resources to effectively carry out their role in the cure of souls. Many suddenly found themselves occupying a "downtown" location. Their memberships were no longer isomorphic with geographical districts. Even neighborhood churches composed of distinct ethnic or economic groups couldn't claim to represent the whole community or even a representative cross section. The churches' responsibilities for ministering to the needs of an urban population were as amorphous as their demographic boundaries. Over what domain were the churches to exercise their guidance? To whom should their members direct mutual edification or fraternal correction?

Spiritual counselors knew what they were calling people from, but few had any idea what to call them to. Culture lag had set into church life, creating what intellectual historian Arthur Schlesinger deems "the critical period" in American religious thought. Church ministry had failed "to adjust to the unprecedented conditions created by rapid urban and industrial growth. American Protestantism, the product of a rural, middle class society, faced a range of problems for which it had neither the experience nor the aptitude."[12]

Those afflicted with American nervousness were understandably alienated from the nation's "official" religion.

Traditionally, religion is the prime source of guiding symbols and healing rituals which together maintain harmony between the individual and the wider social environment. As cultural anthropologist Anthony Wallace points out:

> When a person's identity is unsatisfactory, ritual is a source to which he may turn in order to achieve salvation. Most if not all cultures recognize at least some such identity problems and prescribe culturally standardized ways . . . to achieve relief.[13]

Unfortunately such was not the case for Americans during this critical period of the nation's religious life, for by the 1860s even revivalism had lost much of its suasive power. Popular fascination with science undercut confidence in traditional theological explanations of the Holy Spirit and, by implication, the "plausibility" of instantaneous conversions. American Protestantism had traditionally been reluctant to invoke the supernatural through the means of ritual and sacrament anyway. With the temporary demise of its major institution for personal renewal, revivalism, it now offered precious little to those in need of inner renewal.

Whenever rituals aimed toward personal renewal have been ignored or for any reason become inaccessible to large numbers of individuals, the conditions are ripe for what Wallace refers to as a "revitalization movement." Under these circumstances "a new religious movement is very likely to develop, led by a prophet who has undergone an ecstatic revelation, and aimed at the dual goal of providing new and more effective rituals of salvation and of creating a new and more satisfying culture."[14] In other words, people deprived of ritual are ready to listen to someone who has himself experienced inner cure and is able to teach them the principle behind that healing in the form of a practical philosophy of life.

A revitalization movement is, of course, but another term for what historians of American religion refer to as an awakening. Awakenings, according to William McLoughlin, "are the results, not of depressions, wars, or epidemics, but of critical disjunctions in our self-understanding . . . [from] periods of cultural distortion and grave personal stress."[15] Whether labeled an awakening or a revitalization movement, what we are concerned with here is the process through which a society reintegrates itself by giving new definition to its most treasured beliefs and values. McLoughlin rightfully draws attention to the fact that awakenings are necessary ingredients of social progress. "Insofar as a theological position [here Puritan-inspired Protestantism] is an ideology, that is, gives meaning and order to the lives of a people, it is subject to reinterpretation (or dissolution) in the light of significant changes in the economic, demographic, political, or social affairs of the people who hold it."[16]

As we saw in Chapter 4, mesmerism entered American cultural thought in the ideological wake of the Second Great Awakening which reached its peak about 1830. It was not until 1890 or so that a third such awakening fully reoriented the "culture core" to the forces of modernization. Yet, interestingly enough, the major themes of this eventual religiocultural synthesis were fully anticipated in the mesmerists' therapeutic practices as early as the 1860s. Apparently the intellectual contours of this early psychological system were sufficiently flexible to accommodate to the needs of those affected first and worst by the strains

117

of modern living.[17] To borrow once again from the theoretical scheme proposed by Anthony Wallace, mesmerism gave focus to popular demand for a new and more satisfying world view. It promoted both personal and cultural renewal by producing a prophet who (1) had undergone an ecstatic revelation; (2) successfully formulated this insight concerning human salvation into a practical code; (3) developed ritualized means to communicate his insights or code to others; (4) established an organization to disseminate this new philosophy of life on a widespread basis; and finally (5) provided individuals with experiences through which they might learn, appropriate, and put this new code into practice.[18]

Phineas Parkhurst Quimby (1802–1866) was as unlikely a religious prophet as this nation has yet produced.[19] Blessed by the ecstatic revelation of his own mesmeric cure, Quimby is the rightful father of the many self-help psychologies which to this day help churched and unchurched Americans alike achieve inner wholeness. In his own backwoods way, Quimby was more attuned to American nervousness than was the neurologically trained Beard. Quimby realized straightway that his contemporaries' problems were not those of deficient neural equipment. It was their by now outmoded ideas about human nature which rendered them so psychologically vulnerable. Ironically, the more tenaciously they held to their moral and religious beliefs, the worse off their psyches became. It followed that the surest antidote to American nervousness was to reprogram a patient's maladaptive world view. Quimby's genius was that he recognized that the science of animal magnetism could be adapted to allow for this expanded view of psychological care and guidance.

The modifications that he introduced into mesmerist doctrine provide a perfect example of what Max Weber calls
the "rationalization" of religious beliefs and practices into
a more encompassing orientation to life. Quimby elevated
mesmerism beyond an ad hoc healing ritual. He showed
his patients how the principle behind mind cure furnished
important clues to the secret of successful living. By expanding mesmerist psychology into a total philosophy of
life, Quimby opened up a whole new era in the American
cure of souls.

In 1838 Charles Poyen stopped in Belfast, Maine, on his
proselytizing tour through New England. There a young
and inquisitive Phineas Quimby sat spellbound while
Poyen demonstrated the astonishing powers of animal
magnetism. After the demonstration Phineas fairly as-
saulted Poyen with questions about this mysterious mental
fluid. Poyen obliged the young clockmaker and gratu-
itously added that he, too, could develop mesmeric powers if he but applied himself. Quimby's mind was instantly
resolved. He set his other duties aside and followed Poyen
from town to town until he at last mastered the theory and
practice of animal magnetism. In no time at all he was
practicing on his own, beginning what was to be a twenty-
eight-year career in mental healing.

It was Quimby's good fortune to soon meet up with a
young man by the name of Lucius Burkmar. Lucius was
a particularly adept trance subject and, in this capacity, assisted Quimby in demonstrating mesmerism before large
audiences. Lucius displayed all of the usual mesmeric phenomena, including the capacity for clairvoyance and telepathy. After he placed Lucius into the mesmeric state,
Quimby directed him to use his clairvoyant powers to di-

agnose people's illnesses and then prescribe a medicinal remedy to rejuvenate their vital fluids. On many occasions Quimby dispensed with Lucius' assistance and instead transmitted magnetic energies from his own brain directly into the patient's body. The two methods were clearly distinguishable. The one dependent upon Lucius' diagnosis and prescription eventually elicited the patient's own commitment to a regimen of cure which in itself seemed to comply with standard medical assumption concerning the nature of disease and cure. The other method relied solely upon Quimby's psychic ability to effect a change in the patient's physical system. Yet, to Quimby, both rested upon his belief that "the phenomenon was the result of animal magnetism, and that electricity had more or less to do with it."[20] Quimby's muddled explanations notwithstanding, cures abounded. Newspapers began to take note, and soon the magnetic doctor from Belfast was being touted as the world's leading mesmerist.

With the passage of time Quimby became increasingly skeptical that animal magnetism alone could be responsible for all his therapeutic successes. It soon dawned on him that Lucius might not be diagnosing the patient's ailment at all. Quimby thought it more likely that Lucius was "merely" using his telepathic powers to read patients' minds. In this way Lucius was able to learn what the patients already believed to be the cause of their troubles. His "accurate" diagnoses so utterly astonished patients that they put their full confidence in his curative powers. Thus the herbal remedies Lucius prescribed worked more upon what the patient believed about his problems than the actual physical disorder. Besides, most of the remedies were innocuous substances that proved equally effective on any of a number of ailments. On one occasion Quimby actually substituted a less expensive substance for the costly one Lucius had suggested—and the patient recovered just the same!

Anyone might have deduced that the patients' beliefs and expectations were at least partially responsible for their rapid recoveries, but Quimby arrived at the more radical conclusion that their illnesses had been caused by their ideas or beliefs in the first place. He said that our minds are the sum total of our beliefs and that, if a person is "deceived into a belief that he has, or is liable to have a disease, the belief is catching and the effects follow from it."[21] Actually Quimby wasn't the first American mesmerist to suggest the psychological origin of physical illnesses. He was, however, far less materialistic in his conceptualization of psychosomatic interaction than his magnetic predecessors. He moved mesmerism one step closer to modern psychiatry by specifically identifying faulty ideas— not magnetic fluids—as the root cause of American nervousness. Or, in Quimby's words, "all sickness is in the mind of belief . . . to cure the disease is to correct the error, destroy the cause, and the effect will cease."[22]

By 1865 nearly twelve thousand patients had made the pilgrimage to Quimby's door. Most came out of sheer desperation only after medical physicians had given up hope of cure. His records show them to have been previously diagnosed as suffering from almost every sort of illness: consumption; smallpox; cancer; lameness; diptheria; and, of course, the many symptoms of American nervousness. Quimby didn't let the small problem that he knew nothing about human physiology deter him. What difference did physiological details make if he was correct in attributing all physical trouble to misguided thinking? "Disease is what follows an opinion, it is made up of mind diverted by error."[23] False reasoning, whether engaged in consciously or unconsciously, misdirects the mind's invisible forces. Quimby believed that it was his responsibility "to come in contact with your enemy, and restore you to health and happiness. This I do partly mentally and partly by talking till I correct the wrong impression and establish the Truth, and the Truth is the cure."[24]

It is important to note that Quimby's mentalistic theory of human illness was not the final cause explanation which many of his interpreters have mistaken it to be. He only accredited our beliefs with being an intervening variable. He held that the real source of human health was the magnetic fluid, or vital force, flowing into the human nervous system from some deeper level of the mind. Beliefs function like control valves or floodgates. They either connect or disconnect the conscious mind from its unconscious depths. "Disease," Quimby insisted, "is the effect of a wrong direction given to the mind."[25] Whenever persons identify themselves solely in terms of outer conditions, they have placed their minds at the mercy of noxious external stimuli. As long as the mind is reacting to sensations received through the physical senses, it is unreceptive to the in-flow of magnetic forces. And, depleted of its proactive energies, the body eventually lapses into disease.

Quimby was at last in position to rid himself of Lucius. His new understanding of mesmerism made it the healer's business to engage clients on a one-to-one basis. "Partly mentally and partly by talking," Quimby tried to overcome his patients' self-defeating attitudes. The so-called mental part was a straightforward application of mesmerism. For example, he cured his brother-in-law of both a lame knee and typhoid fever solely through use of mesmeric passes.[26] Similar treatments were reported by others: "I was not treated [verbally] but by rubbing and through mesmerism"; "The treatment was entirely by manipulation. I never, in the different times that I visited him, heard him mention God in any way"; "He never told me how he healed, but employed rubbing [i.e., brisk mesmeric passes] in my case."[27] These treatments were, as we shall see, rather atypical. Most patients were given both a dose of animal magnetism and one of "talking."

Quimby's practices actually resembled those of a shaman more closely than those of a modern psychotherapist. He began treatment by entering into a self-induced, altered state of consciousness resembling that which mesmerists called the state of "extraordinary lucidity."[28] While in this superior mental state, he claimed to "see" a psychic atmosphere enveloping his patients' physical bodies. Quimby explained that a person's magnetic fluids "create around them a vapor. And in that vapor are all the ideas right or wrong."[29] Quimby could thus claim to know his patients better than they knew themselves. There was a metaphysical literalism to his insistence that long-forgotten incidents or rarely articulated opinions continued to linger on in his patients' mental atmospheres. His facility in using the mesmeric state of consciousness for the purpose of diagnosis put him into instant rapport with a stratum of mental life about which they were largely unaware.

Treatment consisted in reenergizing the invisible mental atmosphere. Quimby's tutelage under Poyen had prepared him to perform the mesmeric feat of "daguerreotyping" magnetic fluids into his clients' minds. He sat silently with his patients and, through sheer intensity of psychic effort, transmitted healing forces from his own person onto the receptive plate furnished by their mental atmospheres. His mesmerically acquired telepathic powers made it possible for him to implant images of health directly into his patients' subconscious minds. There, firmly embedded in the mental atmosphere, these images could then materialize themselves in the physical body. "I can impart something from my mind that can enter into that distressed state of fluids and change the heat and bring about a healthy state."[30]

Quimby employed a variety of mesmeric practices to help quicken the flow of animal magnetism in his clients' psychic systems. For instance, he often told his patients to hold a pitcher of water while he rubbed the afflicted parts of their body. He occasionally directed them to swallow small amounts of this water at stated intervals throughout the treatment. This practice, probably picked up from Poyen, dates back to the French mesmerist Deleuze, who was the first to note that "magnetized water is one of the most powerful and salutary agents that can be employed. It conveys the magnetic fluid directly to the stomach, thence into all the organs."[31] When asked to explain why he dipped his hands into water before beginning his passes, Quimby matter of factly replied that water was "a good conductor of vital energy, and when the hands are wet the current flows better from the treater to the patient."[32] Whether this practice rested on fact or superstition, one thing was for sure—it made particularly innovative use of the Christian rituals of water baptism and the laying on of hands. Highly symbolic in their own right,

Quimby's gestures undoubtedly heightened the expectation that wonderful and mysterious changes were about to take place.

The explanations Quimby offered for his healing powers often defy rational interpretation. For example, he claimed to travel clairvoyantly into the "land of darkness with the light of liberty, [to] search out the dungeons where the lives of the sick are bound, enter them and set the prisoners free."[33] It is a difficult hermeneutic issue whether this is to be taken literally or figuratively. Perhaps Quimby didn't know himself. He lacked a vocabulary with which to communicate the paranormal features of mesmeric cure. In a fit of exasperation he once confessed, "I cannot find language to express this so you will understand it."[34] When a gentleman made him an offer of one thousand dollars for the secret behind his cures, he was forced to reply, "I can't, I don't understand it myself."[35] He wrote one person: "I do not know much more about it than you. There is nothing occult about it that I know of. I simply know that I have this power given to me. I do not understand what it means, do not know what it is, or where it comes from."[36] Quimby's appreciation for the ineffable dimensions of mesmeric cure was a far cry from his followers' later claim to know everything about the powers of the subconscious mind.

There was only one problem with mental treatment: It didn't always work. True, mesmeric treatments often gave instantaneous relief from ailments which had been deemed incurable. But in many cases the symptoms reappeared a few days later. It seems that most of Quimby's patients were in need of something a bit more thoroughgoing. Daguerreotyping additional magnetic energies into their mental atmospheres did nothing to rectify the circumstances which had rendered them vulnerable in the first place. Quimby soon learned that he had to talk his clients into redirecting their mental efforts. Quimby said of himself that he used "his clairvoyant faculties to get knowledge in regard to the disease which does not come through his sense, and by explaining it to the patient gives another direction to the mind and this explanation is the science or the cure."[37] His logic here is not unlike that which prompted Freud to first supplement hypnotic treatment and then finally abandon it altogether in favor of psychoanalysis. Momentary relief from internal tensions is not synonymous with cure. Patients also need to achieve conscious insight into the nature and origin of their difficulties. In a modern, pluralistic society mental healing entails putting a client in touch with a more constructive orientation toward managing life's difficulties. As Erik Erikson observed, the modern clinician must also "have some theories and methods which offer the patient a whole world to be whole in."[38]

Prior to Quimby, neither medical physicians nor conventional mesmerists were really prepared to treat persons whose problems couldn't be reduced to organic disorders or a simple lack of inner drive. For their part, nineteenth-century physicians had been trained under a medical philosophy often referred to as materia medica. As a model of the human organism, materia medica knew nothing of psychosomatic interaction. Physicians tended to look at mental and emotional disorders as ephemeral if not downright hypochondriacal. Doctors didn't consider it their task to treat complaints for which no obvious physical cause could be found. Nor were they about to encourage self-indulgence by allowing their patients to freely vent personal frustrations. The bottom line in all of this was that nineteenth-century Americans were unlikely to find the medical profession of much help when it came to treating the root causes of American nervousness.

One of Quimby's patients cut to the very quick of the matter when he admitted that, even though he had visited several doctors and mesmerists, "in no instance did I get rid of all my ailments, because I had not been helped out of the error in which opinions involve us."[39] In other words, someone had had to help save him from himself. Restrictive self-concepts needed to be discarded to make room for a more satisfying philosophy of life. In the long run, moral or ethical guidance was a more essential ingredient of mental health than was the inner glow obtained during mesmeric therapy. The nervous American required guidance concerning how he might establish more productive relationships with both God and neighbor. Quimby not only expanded the scope of mesmeric cure to make these cognitive adjustments available to his clients, he fairly rammed them down their throats.

Quimby was quick to realize that "in fact the theory of correcting diseases is the introduction to life."[40] The science of animal magnetism was implicity a Science of Life. This was quite a compliment in a period when the word *scientific* popularly connoted "man can use it." Nineteenth-century Americans interpreted the telegraph, photography, and steam power, all as evidence that nature's invisible energies would eventually satisfy man's every fancy. Quimby actually insisted that what distinguished irrational faith from true religion was that the latter demonstrated itself as a science of cause and effect. To his way of thinking, mesmerist psychology was just such a spiritual science. It proved beyond question that invisible spiritual forces acted upon the human constitution in a lawful or scientific fashion. If he could just show his patients "that a man's happiness is in his belief, and his misery in the effort of his belief, then I have done what never has been done before. Establish this and man rises to a higher state of wisdom, not of this world, but of that World of Science . . . the Wisdom of Science is Life eternal."[41]

The gospel of mind cure had a beautiful simplicity about it. Right beliefs channel health, happiness, and wisdom out of the cosmic ethers and into persons' mental atmospheres. By controlling our beliefs we control the shunting valve connecting us with psychological abundance. The key element, Quimby counseled, was to identify ourselves in terms of internal rather than external reference points. So long as persons believe that the external environment is the only source from which to derive measures of self-worth they will lose contact with their inner, spiritual selves. The human nervous system can not operate solely upon the capricious messages supplied by the physical senses without eventually becoming embroiled in fear, worry, and finally disease. Human misery, then, is the lawful consequence of allowing other persons and outer events to supply us with our sense of self-worth. Or, in Quimby's own words, "disease is something made by belief or forced upon us by our parents or public opinion. . . . Now if you can face the error and argue it down you can cure the sick."[42]

With a dualistic vision straight out of the revivalists' handbook, Quimby decreed that "there are two sciences, one of this world, and the other of a spiritual world, or two effects produced upon the mind by two directions."[43] In other words, mesmerist psychology empirically verified Americans' belief that humans possess both a lower, animal nature and a higher, spiritual nature. Yet the difference between the two could now be expressed in psychological rather than scriptural or theological terms. By turning the mind inward toward its own psychic depths, men and women are, for the first time, in a position to apprehend the true purpose or design behind their otherwise amorphous lives. The Scientific Man is one who has become a medium of higher, spiritual forces. His mind is attuned to the First Cause behind every event in nature. No longer caught up in a world splintered by the physical senses, the man of spiritual science is able to detect a higher meaning or power at work in his life.

Lest his clients fail to see the religious import of Mind Cure Science, Quimby made sure to spell it out for them. Theological doctrines were to be psychologized so as to better square with the phenomenon of mental cure. He taught his patients to recognize God as "invisible wisdom which fills all space, and whose attributes are all light, all wisdom, all guidance and love."[44] Reconciling ourselves with God's emanative spirit is a function of psychological self-adjustment. No other mediator is needed. The doctrine of Christ was thus both a folly and a stumbling block. The Christ "is the God in us all . . . the Christ or God in us is the same that was in Jesus, only in greater degree in Him."[45] Jesus himself predicted that greater things than these we shall do also; Mind Cure Science would instruct us how.

Education, or more precisely re-education, became the principal focus of mind cure healings. "I always found that

129

when I could get the patients clear from their opinions they would express themselves in as strong terms as I had."[46] It was the healer's responsibility "to make war with what comes in contact with health and happiness."[47] Quimby not surprisingly stated that the two "opinions" most inimical to human wholeness were Calvinist theology and materia medica. Time and time again his patients expressed "a most bitter feeling towards physicians and religious teachers."[48] Medical and religious authorities were perceived as advocating fairly rigid moral standards. In a more pluralistic setting these ethical codes were difficult to maintain or, for that matter, even want to maintain. Quimby lashed out at both the ministry and the medical community for stifling his clients' self-expression with what he termed an "established morality." Neither religious supranaturalism nor medical materialism adequately pictured human wholeness. These doctrines failed to square with the psychological laws of cause and effect and were for this reason derisive. "Between both," Quimby railed, "they have nearly destroyed body and soul. One pretends to look after the body and the other the soul."[49]

Quimby boasted that his mind cure theory "never separates our being into fragments." His explanation of health and illness was for this reason a truly Christian Science. It showed how human nature completes itself by inwardly identifying with God's emanative powers. Psychological laws of cause and effect teach us our true identity and thereby constitute a new source of religious faith. They give specificity to an area of life formerly ruled by superstition. No longer need matters concerning our spiritual destiny be set aside as either incomprehensible or dependent upon the fickle ways of God. Quite the contrary. Mind cure psychology proved beyond dispute that God "sanctions men's acts according to their beliefs, and holds them responsible for their beliefs right or wrong without respect to persons."[50]

Quimby had thus managed to psychologize the Protestant ethic. His philosophy of mind cure continued to affirm the intimate connection between religious conviction and material prosperity, but did so by shifting inward the realm in which one is to be held accountable. Quimby posed a world view which, like other pantheistic philosophies espoused during this period, struck out against "the republician idealism of the Protestant ethic with the damage it inflicted upon individuals in an urban and industrial age."[51] The mind cure approach to religious and material well-being was far more democratic. Everyone holds dominion over his own psychological realm. Quimby seemed to be saying that, even if modernity has stripped every other area of life from the range of personal control, we can at least adjust ourselves. In the mind cure scheme this was more than sufficient. Right thinking, accompanied by occasional moments of silence for the purpose of inculcating the inflow of dynamic personal energies, was thought to lawfully connect self-control with physical prosperity. This psychologized rendering of the Protestant ethic had one more advantage over its theological predecessors. In it the unchurched had equal, if not even greater, access to the life abundant.

Mesmerists who continued to rely solely upon mental treatment were a dying breed. Their theories and methods had been pathetically outmoded by the sophistication of modern life. It was only when Quimby decided to supplement mesmeric manipulation with some "talking" that the science of animal magnetism fully addressed itself to the root causes of American nervousness. Quimby had quite unwittingly inaugurated an entirely new social mechanism for treating intrapsychic conflict. For the very first time Americans had recourse to religious counseling outside of an ecclesiastical context.

Historians of American psychology have failed to accredit Quimby's practice of mind cure for its role in the early development of psychotherapy. Like the many American psychotherapies which were to follow in its wake, mind cure provided demoralized individuals with: (1) an intense relationship or rapport with a significant other; (2) a special interpersonal setting believed to be conducive to cure; and (3) a rationale or theory describing illness and health in a way that helped to make sense of everyday life.[52] Quimby was blessed with the rare virtue of being able to put other people at ease. His patients were overwhelmed by his interest and compassion for their difficulties. Many remarked that his eyes communicated a deep acceptance of their personal problems. What is more, he actually listened, something which ministers and doctors weren't prone to do with persons complaining of mental infirmity. With Quimby they were free to honestly explore their feelings and beliefs in a way that wasn't possible with friends, let alone clergymen. Quimby's office provided what sociologists call a sanctioned retreat from the demands and expectations which society ordinarily imposes on us. There, set apart from workday reality, patients were free to let down their outer facades. Sitting peacefully while Quimby performed his mesmeric gestures, many allowed themselves the luxury of focusing upon their deeper thoughts and feelings. This experience of release and re-

newal made it possible for persons to regard themselves
in a more positive light. They could now know, in an almost visceral way, that they possessed personal worth independent of the opinions of others.

But where Quimby differed most from his mesmeric
predecessors was his determined effort to see that his patients understood the principle behind their cure. He
found that "by explaining it to the patient [I give] another
direction to the mind, and this explanation is the science
or cure."[53] However absurd Quimby's ramblings might
strike us today, they can be positively credited with giving
his patients the opportunity to talk about a range of problems for which neither the periods' theology nor medical
science had an appropriate vocabulary. Mesmerist psychology assigned labels to otherwise amorphous troubles.
Vague sources of discontent could finally be placed within
a self-consistent framework and thus made amenable to
further analysis and control.

Quimby's harangues concerning the right and wrong directions of the mind introduced significant modifications
in what psychologist Jerome Frank refers to as a patient's
world view or "assumptive world." It might be said that
an assumptive world consists of those beliefs which we
hold so deeply we aren't even aware of holding them. It
consists of a person's "set of more or less implicit assumptions about himself and the nature of the world he lives
in."[54] Our assumptive world thus provides us with implicit
understandings about how reality operates and, in turn,
shapes our judgment concerning what is or is not appropriate in a given situation. To the degree that these assumptions accurately represent reality, they enhance both
our efficiency and subjective enjoyment of life. Quimby's

patients, however, were suffering precisely because their "opinions" and "beliefs" no longer corresponded to the larger social environment. The assumptive systems they had inherited from earlier generations failed to make adequate sense of either interpersonal or intrapersonal experience. According to Frank, the common element in all modern psychotherapies is that they in some way help bring about appropriate changes in an individual's cognitive orientation. This is, of course, precisely what the "talking" part of Quimby's cures did. His crude psychological terminology supplied nervous Americans with completely new assumptions about the ontology of psychic life. They learned from Quimby that the mind has resources of its own independent of the confusing public sphere. Mesmerist psychology showed them that the true or ultimate source of all good things in life could be found within.

Quimby's psychological guidance differed from contemporary psychotherapy in at least one important respect. He assumed responsibility for teaching his patients how to take a spiritual outlook on life. He took it upon himself to "make war" and "argue down" any religious or moral concept which he believed to be psychologically unsound. He literally browbeat patients into accepting his philosophy for enhancing self-control. Many needed little cajoling before seeing the wisdom in a philosophy promising them transcendence over the harsher things in life. Quimby reassured them that "there is no intelligence, no power or action in matter itself, that the spiritual world to which our eyes are closed by ignorance or unbelief is the real world, that in it lie all the causes for every effect visible in the natural world, and that if this spiritual life can be revealed to us, in other words, if we can understand ourselves, we shall then have our happiness or misery in our own hands; and of course much of the suffering of the world will be done away with."[55]

Mesmerist psychology afforded an assumptive world all its own. Mental and emotional cure were, in the final analysis, synonymous with internalizing the mesmerists' doctrines as the new basis for self-organization. A typical instance is found in this testimony given by a woman who sought Quimby out after

> six years of great suffering, and as a last resort, after all other methods of cure had utterly failed to bring relief. I had barely faith enough to be willing to go to him, as I had been greatly prejudiced, and still had more of doubt and fear than expectancy of receiving help. . . . It was like being turned from death to life, and from ignorance of the laws that governed me to the light of truth, in so far as I could understand the meaning of his explanations. . . . He continued to explain my case day to day, giving me some idea of this theory and its relation to what I had been taught to believe, and sometimes sat silently with me for a short time [i.e., quietly daguerreotyping mesmeric energies onto her unconscious mental atmosphere].[56]

These sessions continued until she let go of the theological notion that her sufferings represented God's displeasure with her personal shortcomings. Quimby's unique combination of silent animal magnetic treatments and educative guidance finally brought about a total mind cure:

> The general effect of these quiet sittings with him was to light up the mind, so that one came in time to understand the troublesome experiences and problems of the past in light of his clear and convincing explanations.

I remember one day especially, when a panorama of past experiences came before me, and I saw just how my trouble had been made; how I had been kept in bondage and enslaved by the doctors and the false opinions that had been given me. From that day the connection was broken with these painful experiences and . . . I lived in a larger and freer world of thought.[57]

Cure of this kind dealt a fatal blow to the simple practice of mesmerism. Quimby and his disciples set loose an ideological current which brushed aside concern for the mesmeric state of consciousness. Mesmerist psychology was no longer so much a healing ritual as it was a philosophy of the good life. Even its name was lost in the transition; thereafter mesmerism was called mind cure philosophy or the New Thought. What was formerly an explanation of the healing process was now a program for mentally commanding subconscious energies into the service of the whole personality. The mind cure version of mesmerist psychology had a new curative function all its own. It reduced the complex social order to eminently manageable proportions. Those Americans too confused to make adjustments in the outer world could instead set about adjusting themselves.

In its own peculiar way, the mind cure system came to perform for the American cure of souls what Puritan piety had in an earlier cultural setting. It defined a particular lifestyle believed to be in objective correspondence with the invisible spiritual order of things. And with the advent of mind cure philosophy Americans for the first time had access to a self-help spirituality in the form of popular psychology.

Chapter 6

Psychology as Popular Philosophy

To come into the full realization of your awakened interior powers is to be able to condition your life in exact accord with what you would have it.
—Ralph Waldo Trine, 1897

Quimby died in 1866, and for all intents and purposes so did the practice of American mesmerism. Quimby's followers turned out to be far more interested in "talking" away mental disorders than in dispersing them through mesmeric hand gestures. Insight into the psychological causes of human suffering inspired them to find ways of thinking away all the problems that currently nagged the American spirit. The most famous of Quimby's disciples, Mary Baker Eddy, turned mind cure nomenclature into one of our country's largest native-born religions. She had arrived, a helpless cripple, at Quimby's doorstep in 1862. The wiley old gentleman from Belfast healed her afflicted body and, in the process, stuffed her receptive mind full of new ideas. Once healed, Mrs. Eddy resolved that she, too, could take up a career in mental healing. Her first public lecture, "P. P. Quimby's Spiritual Science Healing

Disease as Opposed to Deism or Rochester-Rapping Spiritualism," made her the movement's first spokeswoman. Unfortunately, no sooner had she begun to master her role as dispenser of metaphysical truths, when her source of inspiration suddenly passed away.

Quimby's death temporarily robbed Mary Baker Eddy of her newly found confidence. No longer able to rely on the support of her mentor, she had no other choice but to put her faith in the interior powers about which he had spoken so much. She paid her final respects in a poem entitled "Lines on the Death of P. P. Quimby, Who Healed with the Truth that Christ Taught in Contradistinction to All Isms," and resolved to carry the message forward by herself. All she had left was a manuscript scribbled from Quimby's notes and vague memories of his references to the principles of a real Christian Science. From that point until her death in 1910, Mrs. Eddy worked incessantly at giving literary, theological, and eventually even ecclesiastical embodiment to the science of mental healing.[1] While hers is not our story, it does exemplify how fully mesmerist psychology melded with American Protestantism's tendency to spill over into programs of inner-sanctification and moral self-improvement.

The twenty years immediately following Quimby's death were crucial ones for determining his final legacy to American religious thought. During this period Quimby's practices continued to evolve into a full-blown philosophy of life, prompting the movement's self-appointed historian to designate this as the Mental Science or Mind Cure stage in the development of his teachings.[2] The period is demarcated by the efforts of three of Quimby's other disciples, who prevailed over and against Mrs. Eddy

mind's hidden resources lived in the city.[3] Many of them had only recently arrived from smaller towns and were still seeking ways to adjust to an urban environment. Their names reflect little ethnic diversity, with most suggesting white, Anglo-Saxon, Protestant descent. It also seems safe to infer that the majority were drawn from the middle or even upper-middle classes, since new recruits were inclined toward attending lectures and setting aside large blocks of time for independent reading. Moreover, mind cure appealed to women over men by a ratio of almost two to one. Middle-class women in the late nineteenth century had much more leisure time and far fewer constructive outlets for their energies than did their male counterparts.[4] The only role open to them, that of the housewife, was being further diminished by the forces of modernization. The family unit was gradually losing its economic and emotional cohesiveness—a process they were powerless to arrest. Many, quite understandably, found themselves incapacitated by psychosomatic ailments. Mind cure provided a new outlet for their involuted energies. It got them out of their homes and in touch with people who would listen sympathetically and then coax them into discovering interesting new things about themselves. By attending lectures and enrolling in further course work, they quickly knew as much about this exciting medical and religious breakthrough as anybody. In a period in which neither businesses nor churches encouraged women to aspire to roles of leadership, mind cure was a new field in which they might express their otherwise uncultivated potential.

An investigation conducted in the 1890s probed further into the reasons for public interest in mental healing. A Clark University psychologist by the name of Henry Goddard set out to shed light on what was fast becoming a controversial issue in the religious and scientific communities alike. Goddard distributed questionnaires, conducted interviews, observed healing sessions, and waded through hundreds of case reports supplied him by cooperative metaphysical healers. Out to win respect for the "new psychology" just then emerging in American universities, Goddard expressed pleasant surprise over finding so much evidence indicating the efficacy of nonmedical healings. He concluded that "we have abundant experimental proof of the value of mental practice for the cure of disease . . . we are convinced that it is impossible to account for the existence of these practices if they did not cure disease, and if they cured disease it must have been the mental element that was effective. It is not a thing of the day; it is not confined to a few; it is not local."[5]

Goddard observed an important and clear-cut difference between the Christian Science healers he interviewed and those following in the path of Quimby, Evans, and the Dressers. The latter weren't wedded to a dogmatic theology and were, thus, much more willing to discuss their cases. Many freely admitted numerous failures and realized that, while their methods worked for certain patients, they had little or no effect on others. Most of them were openly self-critical and seemed willing to entertain alternative explanations for their failures and successes—a far cry from the gullible lot he had expected them to be.

There remained the problem of interpretation. Since so much depended upon the credibility of the proffered diagnoses, Goddard tried wherever possible to restrict his interpretations to those cases for which a trained medical physician had submitted a supportive affidavit. Acknowledging an inescapable degree of ambiguity, he estimated that 33 percent of the mind curists' patients received instant cures, 50 percent evidenced gradual healings, while about 17 percent had nothing to show for their money. The successful cures included cases of deafness, lengthening of legs from one to five inches, alcoholism, hemorrhoids, heart murmurs, nervous disorders, and assorted respiratory and digestive problems. Without bothering to enlighten us concerning the thorny issue of how withered limbs could be made to grow several inches, Goddard ventured his opinion that mental healing proved efficacious only in those cases where the illness had been of a functional rather than organic nature. He concluded that, although the mind curists utilized an outmoded terminology in referring to their practices, they had performed a great service to the scientific community by demonstrating the existence and therapeutic utility of a "psychical region that is not in full view of the ordinary consciousness, the so-called subliminal consciousness."[6] Goddard was certain that before long academic psychology would replace the mind curists' incipient supernaturalism with a thoroughly rationalistic account of the subliminal state of consciousness. In the meantime he conceded that "Mental Science, or the New Thought . . . seems to teach a sound philosophy and much practical sense in regard to therapeutics. . . . It is worthy of praise, help, and encouragement."[7]

The questionnaire responses included in Goddard's report show that the mind curists' patients had learned to attribute strikingly similar meanings to illness and health. Before their cure they had believed that matter (i.e., large government, crowded streets, social mores, unloving spouses) had the power to inflict emotional damage. It was as though matter had an intelligence and causal force of its own. Mental healing proved these assumptions false. Their cures convinced these patients that their troubles had quite literally been all in their heads. Since happiness and misery proved to be governed by intrapsychic laws of cause and effect, they at last found themselves always in a position to take control of their lives. The moment they overcame the illusion of the outer senses and began to shift their identities inward, they no longer felt so weak and vulnerable. Feelings of lack and limitation had been dispelled by belief in the potency of mind over matter. The testimonies are most instructive:

> Took some treatments off and on for two years, but growingly, the greater normality of self-healing dawned upon me . . . I intuitively became thoroughly idealistic and optimistic. Knowledge of the creative power of thought stood before me as the one great truth needed to cure the woes of the world. But the supra-naturalism of the church and the materialism of science made and still make both hostile to such a philosophy. A feeling of at-one-ment with the Universal Goodness may be systematically cultivated and may be depended upon to displace all opposites. I became convinced that these things are all law, as exact as any law of physics or chemistry.

> I learned to lean upon the ALL WITHIN myself. Progress was slow (but there was a life time of weakness to overcome) but the improvement was noticeable from the very first treatment . . . I listen to the Kingdom of the ALL WITHIN me for the wisdom that never fails. This is the most essential thing I have learned in Mental Science, and this has the greatest influence upon my life. There are millions and millions of forces awaiting our

recognition and if we hold ourself receptive to this truth, there is no limit to our growth.[8]

Recovery and the internalization of the mind curists' theories seemed to go hand in hand. Healing was experienced as an adjustment in one's metaphysical—rather than physical or psychological—being. Patients enthusiastically attributed their dramatic turnarounds to tides of psychic energy now flowing freely into the subliminal levels of their minds. The mind cure experience had a numinous quality to it that reinforced their conviction that they had inwardly contacted a higher spiritual power. Cured patients walked away from their healings certain that they had been introduced to a whole new approach to life's challenges. It but remained for them to fill in the details of their new belief system by diligently mastering the many terms and definitions which the mind curists used to categorize human experience. One individual candidly revealed that, ever since his mental cure, he had "read almost everything appertaining to psychology during the last few years. Its effect is marvelous. It opens the gateway to health, happiness, serenity, advancement, both spiritual and temporal; develops the intellect, abolishes fear and worry, alters our ideas about Divinity, and gives us more than a glimpse into a future state of existence."[9]

Psychology for this person, as for many Americans in the 1870s, 80s, and 90s, meant the mind curists' endless stream of publications. Scores of articles and books were churned out to condense the principles of mesmeric healing into neatly packaged self-study programs. Transmitting animal magnetism through the printed word drastically increased the numbers who were able to come into contact with its extraordinary powers. It also encouraged ambitious authors to extrapolate healing techniques into formulas that could be applied to most every problem besetting their readers.

The linking of psychological theory with the needs and interests of a general reading audience set mesmerism upon a course that was destined to obscure its earlier uses. The historical process through which mesmerism evolved from a ritual of inner-healing into a program of self-adjustment and then finally into a psychologized philosophy is perfectly chronicled in the movement's literature. These three interpretations or uses of mesmerist psychology respond to distinct chronological stages in mesmerism's passage through American intellectual thought.[10] They can also be viewed as three different levels at which the mesmerists' teachings might be understood. After all, even into the early twentieth century many mind curists continued to concern themselves with describing the mesmeric state of consciousness and the subjective experience of ecstatic self-transcendence.[11] These authors kept the explicitly religious and mystical character of mental healing alive by continuing to identify tingling magnetic vibrations and dazzling streams of white light with divine powers. However, following Quimby's further revelation that "the explanation is the cure," a host of mind curists busied themselves with a second task—that of prescribing right beliefs.[12] What we previously described as the Mental Science or Mind Cure stage in the development of Quimby's teachings witnessed the proliferation of treatises devoted to describing the kind of personality reorganization thought to be indispensable to spiritual renewal. These works formed the literary basis of what came to be known as the New Thought philosophy. By the late 1880s, a third and final type of literature appeared. The later New Thought authors, sometimes referred to as the positive thinkers, attempted to systematically apply mind cure principles to the routine affairs of everyday life.[13] In practice this resulted in an uncritical use of mind cure psychology for deriving surefire solutions to difficulties arising in home life, interpersonal relationships, and business. Books like *Thought Is Power, How to Use New Thought in Home Life, How to Get What You Want,* and *Making Money: How to Grow Success* turned belief in the powers of the mind into a full-blown ideology. In other words, mesmerism eventually evaporated into a fairly uncritical cult of the power of positive thinking.

The progressive attenuation of mesmeric healing into a popular philosophy began with the New Thought's pioneer author Warren Felt Evans. The son of a Vermont farmer, Evans spent a few years at both Middlebury and Dartmouth Colleges before his ordination as a Methodist Episcopal minister. The fact that he went through eleven parish appointments in rapid succession suggests that he wasn't quite cut out for a conventional ministry. Evans finally up and quit to write and lecture for the Swedenborgian Church in America. During all of this his health grew increasingly unsteady. He confessed that "my nervous system had been so prostrated that trembling seizes upon me in the performance of the slightest service."[14] A visit to Quimby in 1863 lifted his internal energies to a higher pitch and simultaneously provided him with a spiritual outlook broad enough to house his restless intellect. Quimby sensed that Evans possessed above-average capabilities and encouraged him to set up his own practice of mental medicine. Evans took Quimby's advice and set himself to the task of ministering to the countless numbers of Americans yearning for a secularized salvation.

Evans opened an office in Claremont, New Hampshire, before moving the base of his operations to Boston. He spent the next twenty years there spearheading the growth of Mind Cure Science. His private healing practice and occasional public lectures contributed a great deal to the dissemination of Quimby's doctrines. It was, however, Evans's pen which ultimately scattered healing vibrations across the continent. His *The Mental Cure* (1869) went through seven editions by 1885; *Mental Medicine* (1871) merited fifteen by the same year. Four other volumes—*The Divine Law of Cure, Esoteric Christianity and Mental Therapeutics, The Primitive Mind Cure,* and *Soul and Body*—carefully explained the science of mental healing as a practical application of Christian metaphysics. His writings all bore the spirit of an author who believed himself to be witnessing the dawn of a new age. "We live in one of those mighty transitory epochs of human history, when old things are becoming new. We are realizing the fulfillment of the prophetic announcement of ages ago, that God would pour out his spirit upon all flesh."[15]

Entering into the New Age consciousness and partaking of God's sacramental dispensations were what mind cure was all about. In true Swedenborgian fashion, Evans conceded that the secrets behind mental healing were as old as Christianity itself. Due to their sublime and esoteric nature, they "had long been occult and withheld from the multitude."[16] It wasn't by happenstance that his *The Primitive Mind Cure* was subtitled "The Nature and Power of Faith or Elementary Lessons in Christian Philosophy and

Transcendental Medicine." He believed that the discovery of the power of mind over matter was, in fact, the kerygma of the early church. The human mind, when rendered susceptible to the influx of magnetic impressions, temporarily gains insight concerning its true spiritual identity. "In the impressible state, the patient comes under the action of the law of faith, the great psychological remedy in the Gospel system, the importance of which even the Christian world has never fully appreciated."[17]

Evans, like Quimby, learned to daguerreotype vital forces into his patients' unconscious minds. "In treating a patient by the mental method, with a kindly positive affirmative attitude of mind, we are to think steadfastly the truth in regard to his inner self, and maintain in our minds the correct idea of ourselves and him; and the silent sphere of our minds according to the law of thought transference, will influence him in a degree proportioned to his susceptibility."[18] Evans also believed that by entering the magnetic state, individuals "come into direct and immediate communication with God that His creative energy shall be added to our cognitive and volitional power."[19]

As valuable as the mental method of cure repeatedly proved itself to be, many patients needed much more than an extra dose of creative energy. Evans agreed with Quimby that patients were never completely cured until they had learned to maintain the "correct idea" about themselves and the world they live in. Furthermore, it wasn't always necessary to help people become susceptible to mesmeric sensations in order to get them to reorganize their personalities. "If the patient is predisposed to believe you, the magnetic state is not necessary to the influence of your affirmations upon him."[20] Informal instruction about the unconscious mind and the "true" laws governing our mental and physical lives could alone help persons to act in accordance with their own higher nature. As Evans's own mentor had put it, the healer's "explanation is the cure; if he succeeds in correcting the error, he changes the fluids of their system and establishes the truth or health. The truth is the cure."[21]

The mind cure view of human nature was thoroughly dualistic. Evans explained how this duality is rooted in the very structure of the brain. One hemisphere of the brain controls our intellectual and volitional function, while the other hemisphere is the seat of our involuntary nature. Evans identified the involuntary portion of the brain as the psychic conduit through which God sends us life and guiding wisdom. So long as we retain a conscious understanding of our total being, our vital bodily processes remain in continuous connection with a wisdom far superior to that of our conscious thoughts. But when, in the course of daily living, we become preoccupied with material conditions or develop a false sense of self-importance, we effectively sever our conscious minds from their unconscious, spiritual source. Evans wrote that we can overcome this inner-duality by shifting our attention inward toward the magnetic or impressible level of consciousness. By "turning the mind inward upon itself towards its divine center, man comes into such relations with his own immortal Self, the anima divina."[22] Here, in what Evans called the preconscious life of the soul, the two hemispheres of the brain are united and restored into "the right relationship of mind to the potent active forces of the universe."[23]

Mental cure was by now synonymous with discovering

the true self. Being fully human meant cutting beneath the many roles and identities foisted upon us by social existence so as to realize the fact that each one of us is inwardly connected to the divine. Evans's description of human nature is in this respect reminiscent of the introspective and ascetic traditions found in either Western gnostic traditions or the meditative paths of both Hinduism and Buddhism. He wrote that the true self is covered over by several sheaths, or layers, of mundane identifications. These must be stripped away before we can ever hope to obtain firsthand knowledge of our own divine nature. "First," he revealed, "is the outer court of sense, next, the inner sanctuary of the intellectual soul; and lastly, in the East, the most holy place, the spirit where like the high priest we may commune with God. This is the inmost region of our being, and our real self. It is included in the Christ, or the Universal Spirit. . . . The Summit of our being which is the real and divine man, is never contaminated by evil, nor invaded by disease."[24]

Evan's description of mental healing trailed off into a normative understanding of human nature. The very fact of mental healing attested to the existence of laws and forces quite superior to those utilized by the average person. Mrs. Eddy put the mind cure mandate into forthright terms when she exhorted her readers to "abandon pharmaceutics and take up ontology—the science of real being."[25] In a similar vein, Evans argued that the only world view which could make adequate sense of the mesmeric state of consciousness was a Christian pantheism.

A Christian pantheism which does not destroy the individuality of man, nor separate God from the universe

150

which he continually creates out of Himself, nor sunder Him from the activities of the human soul by the intervention of second causes, is the highest development of religious thought. An intuitive perception of the unity of the human with the Divine existence is the highest attainable spiritual intelligence, and one which raises man above disease and the possibility of death.[26]

The Emersonian character of mind cure metaphysics was not entirely accidental. Evans was well acquainted with the writings of the Cambridge pundit and shared his Neoplatonic leanings. With Emerson, Evans espoused belief that the individual mind is a potential vessel for an indwelling divinity; that the transcendentally awakened man is the master of his own destiny; that our inner selves correspond to nature's deeper powers; and that all is well even now if we but expand our spiritual vision. The affinity between mind cure and transcendentalism was not, however, owing to any conscious borrowing. Rather, both were deeply rooted in the Swedenborgian legacy to the countervailing forces in American spirituality. The parallels between the two movements attest to the often-obscured symmetry between highbrow and middlebrow cultures. Mesmerist psychology was, by its very nature, a kind of reified doctrine of correspondence. The microcosm, or human psyche, is in a predetermined harmony with the powers that activate the macrocosm. Students of mind cure, by establishing a rapport between their conscious and subconscious selves, could in turn direct powerful cosmic forces. Mind cure was, in its own right, an almost textbook example of what historian Sydney Ahlstrom terms harmonial religion. That is, mesmerist doctrines provided the mind cure authors with a form ". . . of piety and belief in which spiritual composure, physical health, and even economic well-being are understood to flow from a person's rapport with the cosmos."[27]

The mind curists' pantheistic ontology made conventional theology more or less irrelevant. The only barrier separating individuals from spiritual abundance was understood to be a psychological one. In this way, mesmerist theories had done away with the necessity of repentance or contrition as a means of reconciling oneself with God's will. Obedience to the laws of the mind, not to scriptural commandments, is what enables God's presence to manifest itself in our lives. The path of spiritual progress was one of systematic self-adjustment. "In all human endeavor conformity to nature is union with God . . . all the wonderful achievements of modern science and the useful arts—such as telegraphy, photography, and the ten thousand results of machinery—are effected in this way."[28] Mind cure was, thus, a reassuring antidote to nervous exhaustion. Men and women were told to quit straining so hard in their efforts to get ahead in life. Preoccupation with outer conditions ignored the true causal principles governing the universe. It would be far more profitable to spend a few moments alone in silence for the purpose of activating the powers of the unconscious mind. Just beneath the threshold of waking consciousness there exists what Evans termed "a battery and reservoir of magnetic life and vital force" ready to replenish our exhausted nervous systems.[29]

The Dressers' son, Horatio, later explained that mental and physical composure was a matter of how we look at things. "The desideratum is to lift the entire process [of thought] to the spiritual plane, to live in thought with the ideal, to regard mind and body rather from the point of view of the soul, than to look upon the soul from the standpoint of the body."[30] Of course, giving lip service to transcendental vision and actually embodying it were two different things. Practice and a good deal of mental discipline were required. Dresser advised individuals that a good way to begin to acquire a spiritual outlook on life was to read as much about mental science as they possibly could. Slightly more surprising is the fact that many did. Supply and demand escalated throughout the 70s and 80s, as evidenced by the fact that Horatio alone wrote more than thirty books introducing people to their unconscious minds. With a string of books bearing such titles as *Living by the Spirit, The Power of Silence, The Immanent God,* and *Human Efficiency,* Dresser drove home the lesson that God helps those who look within.

Reading was to be supplemented with stated periods of quiet meditation. Mind cure students were taught to sit silently and cultivate the inner sensation of the inflow of psychic energies. In this way, psychological adjustment and inner-sanctification became simultaneous acts of consciousness. Diligent study coupled with periodical moments of mystical reverie accustomed persons to perceiving more than meets the eye. This psychologized understanding of religious virtue was particularly satisfying in an age of rapid social change. Conscientious individuals could systematically apply themselves to the task of developing the ability "to think one's self into a position whence one may look forth upon the universe as veritably a whole ... [wherein] experience will be seen in an entirely different light."[31]

New Thought's most successful author, Ralph Waldo

Trine, made it clear that the mind curists' practices were meeting the needs of the age. Americans were crying out for a "religion that makes for everyday life—adequacy for life. Adequacy for everyday life here and now must be the test of all true religion. We need an everyday, a this worldly religion."[32] To Trine, and the more than two million persons who bought his book, the test of all true religion was whether or not it produced psychological results. More specifically, it must enable us to live "in tune with the infinite." Trine inked the New Thought's rallying cry when he proclaimed:

> The great central fact in human life is the coming into a conscious vital realization of our oneness with the Infinite Life, and the opening of ourselves fully to the Divine inflow. In just the degree that we come into a conscious realization of our oneness with the Infinite Life, and open ourselves to the Divine inflow, do we actualize in ourselves the qualities and powers of the Infinite Life, do we make ourselves channels through which the Infinite Intelligence and Power can work. In just the degree in which you realize your oneness with the Infinite Spirit, you will exchange dis-ease for ease, inharmony for harmony, suffering and pain for abounding health and strength. To recognize our own divinity and our intimate relation to the Universal, is to attach the belt of our machinery to the power-house of the Universe.[33]

Trine viewed mental healing as irrefutable proof that "thoughts are forces." Thoughts generate a vibratory field of energy which can be strengthened and amplified to exert causal influence upon natural conditions. Trine further described that "in the degree that thought is spiritualized, does it become more subtle and powerful . . . this spiritualizing is in accordance with law and is within the power of all."[34] More to the point:

> Within yourself lies the cause of whatever enters your life. To come into the full realization of your awakened interior powers, is to be able to condition your life in exact accord with what you would have it. . . . The realm of the unseen is the realm of causes—the realm of the seen is the realm of effects. . . . This is the secret of all success. This is to come into the possession of inborn riches, into the recognition of undreamed of power.[35]

The New Thoughters were, in effect, advising their readers to adopt mental habits which would duplicate the kind of thinking associated with the mesmeric state of consciousness. It was Evans who first denounced the physical and social worlds of human experience as obstacles to authentic self-actualization. The tangible realms of life continually make demands upon us which inhibit the free expression of our highest mental powers. "The real and immortal man is imprisoned and in chains. It should be our aim to free the living soul from its unnatural subjection to material limitations and teach it to live, even when on earth independent of the body."[36] After all, what was religious faith except the commitment to distrust what the physical senses tell us and, instead, to subscribe to spiritual laws of cause and effect? Evans nurtured his readers' quest for inner-sanctification by manufacturing one article after another, each harping on the divine command to "learn to contradict the senses." Old mental habits had to be broken and new ones substituted before the mind could be elevated above "the plane of sense with its false and deceptive appearances."[37]

Under the direction of Evans and others, the mesmerists' discoveries were being extrapolated into a distinctive philosophical position. The mesmeric state of consciousness had taught them that mind can triumph over matter, subjective desires over objective conditions. The New Thought promised cognitive transcendence over the myriad complications of life. It taught that there was no material need or lack which could not be met by cultivating the proper frame of mind.

Evans, the pioneer, was followed by others anxious to write their way to psychological utopia. Emile Cady's *Lessons in Truth* followed suit with a primer on the subject "Who and What God Is—Who and What Man Is." Defining God as unlimited supply made it axiomatic that religion has to do with claiming our fair share. "That source and you are connected every moment of your existence. You have power to draw upon that Source for all the good you are, or ever will be capable of desiring."[38] Cady further explained that "certain conditions of mind are so connected with certain results that the two are inseparable."[39] It is our thinking which makes for our happiness or unhappiness, our successes or nonsuccesses. Humans are psychologically entitled to divine assistance and anyone but a fool would learn to hold God to his end of the bargain. Cady recommended we begin by setting aside a period of every day for psychological exercise. For warm-ups we ought to relax just enough to permit our attention to shift inward. This practice was often called "entering the silence" and served the practical purpose of strengthening our subconscious connection to the divine mental warehouse.[40] Once this was accomplished, the real workout could start. Several minutes were to be devoted to the constant repetition of verbal formulas which have the ability to deploy the mind's hidden energies to the service of the conscious personality. Statements like "God works in and through me . . . hence I cannot fail," "I am spirit . . . I manifest my real Self now," and "Pain, sickness, poverty, old age, and death cannot master me for they are not real" reminded the mind's creative Source of his convenantal obligations.

"As a man thinketh, so is he" was no mere metaphor for the New Thoughters. It was metaphysical law. Mind cure psychology assured Evans that "if we form the true idea of man and apply it to ourselves, and hold it steadfastly in the mind and believe in its realization, by one of the deepest and most certain laws of our nature, it will tend to recreate the body of that mental type."[41] Some found even Evans's formulation a bit too anemic. A New Thought journal called *The Higher Law* typically described the power of mind over matter in terms of technique. With proper instruction anyone can learn to transcend the limitations of finite thought and begin to "draw power and wisdom at will. . . . The divine presence is known through experience. The turning to a higher plane is a distinct act of consciousness. The power can be used as the sun's rays can be focused and made to do work, to set fire to wood."[42]

Mesmer's discovery had grown more remarkable with age. He had boasted that the vital principle behind innercure effected direct and immediate changes in the nervous system. All other disorders could only be mediately influenced toward the good. His twenty-seven principles implied that psychic powers, even when greatly intensified, are but one of the causal forces which govern objective reality. The New Thoughters were, on the contrary, fully determined to rid the universe of mediating influences of every kind. When they told themselves that "thoughts are forces," they meant just that. Properly spiritualized thoughts could be counted on to daguerreotype desired conditions onto the blank screen of the physical universe. By dipping into their subconscious and conjuring up a state of mysticism and reverie, the New Thought ideologues telepathically transmitted their wishes out into the psychic ethers with full confidence that immutable psychological laws would take care of the details.

The cult of positive thinking continued to build upon the psychological realism with which mesmerism described the mind's invisible powers. Henry Wood best expressed the message attracting readers to New Thought in a volume which he entitled *Ideal Suggestions through Mental Photography.* The reason behind Wood's publishing success was quite simple. He refused to burden his readers with useless chatter about mind cure's earlier concern with spiritual upliftment. "Utility," he constantly reminded himself, "is the watchword of the present age." Mesmeric daguerreotyping, or mental photography as he called it, made the discoveries of the telegraph and electricity pale by comparison. Wood's imagination reeled at the very idea that man's "own thought-power is a force, the intensity and utility of which had been almost undreamed of."[43] Surely this discovery must contain pecuniary importance thus far neglected by well-meaning but insufficiently practical mental healers.

Wood confessed that he had never actually practiced mental healing himself. In fact, he bragged about it. His credentials were the no-nonsense attitudes which had already made him a small fortune in the business world.

Wood wasn't one to forget that demonstrable results, and not endless introspection, were what really counted in life. He explained that the New Thought was "not distinctly a new religion, or even a new healing system, but a new all-inclusive way of life."[44] Wood thought it high time to dispense with all this talk about inner-spirituality and get on with more-important matters like masterminding financial coups. He set about stripping the mind curists' science of its former "technicality and occult terminology," so that others would see it as the utilitarian lifestyle he believed it to be.[45] Streamlined to its essentials, the philosophy of mind cure was "a pure scientific application of well-understood means to ends."[46]

Wood's self-paced instructions for mental photography vividly depicted the immediate cash value of the mesmerists' talk about thought vibrations and invisible mental atmospheres. He insisted that men and women could literally attract success to themselves by making full use of the mind's magnetic forces. Wood taught that the circuitry of the brain could be rewired a bit so as to work somewhat analogously to photography. He reasoned that we can learn to project mental images out into the physical world, where they will then materialize in exact detail. By stuffing our desires deeply into the unconscious mind, "we may grasp and wield its divine forces, and through them assert our supremacy over the kingdom of our rightful domain."[47] Wood apparently believed that God wants nothing more of us than developing the ability to make the outer world a perfect mirror of our own minds.

By the turn of the century, New Thought had thoroughly equated psychology with self-help techniques for creating a success-oriented personality. "Right belief" now translated into magical mantras which dissolved the harsher facts of life into mental putty. The New Thoughters kept insisting that thoughts are forces and much easier to control than external situations. The very titles of the movement's later literature enticed Americans to make autosuggestion their pathway to successful living. For example, Frank Haddock edited a multi-volume "Power Book Library" which covered such lofty territory as *How to Get What You Want, Practical Psychology, The Personal Atmosphere,* and *Power for Success.* The last-mentioned volume, incidentally, detailed Haddock's own "Twenty-eight Lessons in Success Magnetism." Orison Swett Marden's thirty-odd self-development books made him one of the most widely read American authors in his or any other generation. The substance of the New Thoughters' appeal was the hope they kindled that maybe, just maybe, we can all think our way to fortune. Strangely enough, these success-through-right-thinking authors were upholding the work ethic long grown in our nation's religiocultural heritage. Belief in the power of positive thinking was but a psychological variation on the Puritan conviction of the economic potency of disciplined personal character.[48] The major difference was that it was no longer the quality of one's care or conduct toward others which made a person deserving of material reward; now it was the strength of one's thoughts about oneself. Personal desire, not communal duty, motivated the New Thoughters to live in accordance with the divine.[49]

This relentless pursuit of nothing more constructive than self-regimentation has prompted recent commentators to launch scathing attacks on the New Thought philosophy. In his *The Positive Thinkers,* Donald Meyer blames mind cure for its historical role in whetting Americans' appetites for popular psychologies. Meyer faults all psychologized philosophies of the good life with channeling human energies away from ethical conduct and into ephemeral programs of self-indulgence. In a period that called for new levels of strong, politically sensitized ego strengths, the New Thoughters encouraged persons to think about nothing except their own thoughts. In the final analysis, Meyer writes, "it was the genius of mind-cure to discover how the weak might feel strong while remaining weak."[50] Gail Thain Parker has written an intellectual history of mind cure in New England which likewise has little good to say about the movement.[51] In her view, the bottom line on their intellectual ledger shows them to have waged a desperate struggle to make an inherited work ethic endurable in a new and modern setting. The lip service they gave subjects like mysticism and self-discovery was only a way of masking their more pervasive commitment to the cult of success. Parker concludes that the positive thinkers were so uncritically acceptant of regnant New England values that they were neither prepared for nor even very interested in discovering anything radically new about themselves.

There is a good deal of truth in both Meyer's and Parker's verdicts. The indictments they deliver are, however, far too sweeping. Both are guilty of a miscarriage of historical justice by having read backward from the later New Thought materials in their reconstruction of the rise and fall of mind cure ideas. Meyer was understandably put out with twentieth-century Protestantism's failure to articulate a consistent political realism. He surmised that the churches' accommodation to popular psychologies was to blame, and interpreted mind cure accordingly. Parker, who was puzzled by the success authors' phenomenal ability to peddle psychological puff, also failed to differentiate between the very different meanings which mesmerist psychology had for nineteenth-century Americans. Some eighty years ago Horatio Dresser cautioned that it "would be easy for the superficial reader to seize upon thought as the dominant factor . . . and to overlook the spiritual meaning which [Evans] had previously given the term."[52] In this, Dresser is absolutely correct. It is impossible to make an adequate assessment of the movement's contribution to American culture without first making sense of the successive phases and/or levels of the mesmerists' theoretical efforts. A more balanced interpretation must begin by placing the organic development of the mesmerists' healing practices into some kind of broader historical perspective.

Chapter 7

Mesmerism and the American Cure of Souls

Religion in the shape of mind-cure gives to some of us serenity, moral poise, and happiness, and prevents certain forms of disease as well as science does, or even better in a certain class of persons.
—*William James, 1901*

Good stories teach lessons, and mesmerism's is a timely one. In recent years a good deal of attention has been given to the emergence of new and often puzzling religions. Of all our new religions none are quite so baffling as the many cultlike psychotherapies. EST, Scientology, Transcendental Meditation, Jungian study groups, and sundry fascinations with mysticism and altered states of consciousness have kindled a genuinely religious enthusiasm in their followers. It is not uncommon to hear their members claim to have overcome the tensions of secular existence by realigning themselves with higher spiritual powers. The fact that these therapies function outside of an ecclesiastical setting is, I think, not sufficient reason to prevent them from falling under the general category of the religious cure of souls. That is, insofar as their theories and practices lead individuals beyond their own private resources to those which are thought to flow from some transpersonal source, we are justified in subjecting them to the kinds of analysis peculiar to religious historiography.

If anything is certain about these movements, it is that they have their strongest appeal among those to whom the conventional forms of religion no longer appear relevant. What is less easy to ascertain, is whether they are giving their adherents the kind of religious outlook which will adequately meet the challenges of time and community. We simply lack sufficient perspective from which to make unbiased judgments about the long-term consequences of these emergent religious forms. We can, however, make some preliminary observations by examining the historical context out of which our psychotherapies have come to perform distinctively religious functions in modern society. Beginning as it did with the very birth of psychological theory in this country, the story of American mesmerism offers important clues about the possibilities and limitations which popular psychologies have as models for religious self-understanding.

Any final interpretation of mesmerism must take into consideration its ignominious fate. By 1900 mesmerism had quietly and unobtrusively disappeared as a subject of popular interest. Hindsight can pick out two factors which figured into its demise: the further development of scientific psychology and a resurgence in American church life.[1] Much of the early interest in mesmerism was due to its pretensions to be the first scrupulously empirical explanation of the human psyche. In the 1880s and 90s American universities finally recognized psychology as a legitimate field of scholarly investigation and began to foster the professionalization of the discipline. Laboratories, journals, and graduate curriculums demarcated the "new psychology" from its philosophical and theological predecessors. The first generation of university-trained psychologists were eager to demonstrate the superiority of their new science and did so by writing numerous articles denouncing competing theories like mind cure for being wholly speculative and without proper academic credentials. As scientific psychology continued to gain in stature, mesmerism looked ever more like fanciful metaphysics. Those wishing to be at modernity's intellectual forefront forgot all about the mesmeric state of consciousness and moved on to new, if less interesting, psychological theories.

American churches rebounded from their initial confrontation with urbanization with surprising resiliency. Church membership nearly doubled in the last two decades of the nineteenth century—a rate far surpassing the country's overall population growth. The primary reason was that progressive innovations revamped church life enough to assuage the polemic which modern social forces had thrust upon it. A liberalizing trend in both the period's theology and pastoral care made it possible for church members to reconcile their religious heritage with a more sophisticated way of life. The Social Gospel was already germinating in the minds of church leaders; although it never became a major force in American religious life, its very appearance testifies to the period's increasing concern that faith be made relevant to the actual difficulties facing men and women in their daily lives. It was only a few more years before the pastoral counseling movement emerged with the intention of making psychological method a basic tool of religious ministry.

Neither the rise of secular psychology nor the resurgence in church religiosity fully accounts for mesmerism's total dissolution. They merely explain in what directions the disenchanted might turn in its stead. It is important to remember that the mid- to late-nineteenth century witnessed a widescale clash between competing cultural commitments. Science emerged as a very real challenge, even threat, to religious modes of self-understanding. When the clamor subsided, the church was no longer the dominant source from which individuals sought information about how to organize their lives. While many Americans still turned exclusively to Scripture and church tradition for guidance, a growing proportion began to look elsewhere.[2] The fledgling social sciences found themselves in a position to help individuals find realistic guidelines for handling life's difficulties. Secular professions of healing and guidance grew so rapidly that they actually began to compete with pastoral care as the most influential curator of the American psyche.

This bifurcation of psychological healing into pastoral and secular contexts has never been as clear-cut as many assume. The separation is predicated upon the theoretical and practical usefulness of dividing human problems into two distinct conceptual frameworks: theological conceptions, which root human well-being in some transcendent reality, and psychological explanations, which reduce all considerations about humam nature to empirically verifiable laws of cause and effect. The distinction, however, is at best a shadowy one. Religion has always been a matter of voluntary affiliation in the United States. Formerly this amounted to the right to choose which, if any, denomination best suited one's own religious predilections. More recently it has come to center around the individual's decision as to whether he or she will subscribe to the religious hypothesis at all. In a world which has pushed the divine completely out of the legal, economic, and technological spheres, most persons have nowhere else to search for the sacred except within. The modern religious quest is largely an inward search for the psychological foundations upon which faith might rest. It is no coincidence that liberal theologians have tried to revitalize Christian theology by eradicating metaphors of height and geographical transcendence in favor of imagery connoting depth and spiritual immanence. If we can accept the characterization that ours is an era of religious inwardness, then it comes as no surprise that psychological terminology would be inherently suggestive to the modern religious imagination.

Mesmerism was but the first in a long line of American therapies whose theories concerning the secret behind personal renewal have, for certain segments of the general public, functioned as religious symbols. By voicing dissatisfaction both with narrowly conceived science and narrowly conceived theology, mesmerism promised to forge an intellectual synthesis capable of supporting a more sophisticated religiosity. In this respect mesmerism has definite affinities with the many so-called transpersonal psychologies which today form the interface between academic psychology and popular religion. Movements like TM, Scientology, Psychosynthesis, and Silva Mind Control, have as their central tenet belief in the existence of a dimension of psychological reality which transcends the subject-object relationship. To them, individual wholeness has its roots in certain modes of consciousness which defy reduction to the scientific and theological categories which have, since Descartes, rendered the Western world susceptible to spiritual schizophrenia. Since their descriptions of the "further reaches" of human nature don't quite fall into either the scientific or religious categories adhered to by the larger culture, these movements invariably take on the appearance and society-critiquing functions of a cult. By committing the individual to at least the possibility of arriving at new understandings about the nature and meaning of reality, they serve as powerful sources of cultural innovation.

The famed psychic researcher F. W. Meyers, a contemporary of the mind curists, offered a succinct assessment of the religious function which transpersonal psychologies serve in the lives of unchurched Americans. In an address given more than eighty years ago, Meyers explained that the proponents of these theories were drawn from the ranks of those who no longer found Christian doctrine to be a creditable metaphysic. Refusing to passively endure the spiritual impoverishment brought on by the collapse of Christian theology, they were actively searching for new grounds of religious conviction. Meyer's definition of religion is in itself noteworthy. He described it as the individual's "subjective response to the sum of known cosmic laws and phenomena taken as an intelligible whole."[3] In his view, the investigation of paranormal states of consciousness was at root a religious search. Knowledge about the mind's hidden resources added significant new information concerning "the sum of known cosmic laws." What is more, research into the higher reaches of the human psyche could accommodate scientific and religious sentiments within a single metaphysical enterprise. The discovery that human consciousness opens up to a transpersonal realm reveals conclusively that what is sacred, ultimate, and unconditional about life exists on a continuum with what is mundane, preliminary, and conditioned. Successful adaptation to life's everyday challenges is, in this sense, itself spiritually meritorious.

The very first to recognize that the mesmerists' doctrines had opened new possibilities for the modern cure of souls was William James. The eminent psychologist-philosopher was convinced that in metaphysical healing "a wave of religious activity, analogous in some respects to the spread of early Christianity, Buddhism, and Mohammedism, is passing over our American world."[4] James minced no words in pinpointing the reason why a healing-based belief system could so arouse his contemporaries: "Things are wrong with them." The source of their *Weltschmerz?* Their "little private convulsive selves."[5]

James was hardly a disinterested bystander. He, too, had been a lifelong victim of American nervousness. James was well aware of the fact that chronic psychological malaise had its roots in self-defeating beliefs or attitudes. Certain beliefs prevent the conscious personality from making full use of all the energy at its disposal. Scientific materialism, when coupled with conventional religious belief, has the effect of contracting our subjective sense of life to the point where "everything is hollow, unreal, dead . . . nothing is believed in . . . all sense of reality is fled from life . . . nothing penetrates to the quick or draws blood as it were."[6]

Over-contracted personalities must, by definition, learn to expand their mental boundaries so as to become contin-

169

uous with what James called a psychological "more." Mental healing and religious enlightenment were, thus, virtually indistinguishable for James. Both issue automatically from the experiential discovery that "a way is open to us . . . of going behind the conceptual altogether . . . to the more primitive flux of the sensible life for reality's true shape."[7] The crucial factor, according to James, was learning to pierce beneath the arbitrary world of social convention and gain insight into the preconceptual stuff of psychic experience. It is only then that the beleaguered self opens up to the fact that his "present field of consciousness is a center surrounded by a fringe that shades insensibly into a subliminal more. . . . Every bit of us at every moment is part and parcel of a wider self."[8] James appreciated how the mind curists were helping Americans learn this vital lesson. Their theories and techniques told anxious individuals how to connect themselves with divine mind. Knowing this, James surmised, was the difference between defensiveness and aggressiveness, between the need for self-constraint and that of self-actualization. He believed that the movement's cultural impact fell nothing short of a "copious unlocking of energies."[9]

James accredited the mind curists with propagating a psychological doctrine perfectly adapted to the spiritual needs of his contemporaries.[10] Defending mind curists against those who viewed them as self-abasing automatons, he proclaimed them to be a "psychic type to be studied with respect." In his famous Gifford lectures, James preserved their contributions to American religious life for all posterity. Not only did he hold up mind cure as the paradigmatic expression of the healthy-minded form of religion, he also argued that it was the only species of this type which had proved itself competent to conquer the evil in human experience.

As a philosopher, James was well aware of the difficulty of evaluating religious beliefs. The only criterion he felt could justifiably be used to measure the relative merits of a belief was its adequacy as a guide to practical conduct. Beliefs must structure our activities in ways that contribute to the empirical unification of our incomplete and evolving universe. As for the mind cure hypothesis? "The plain fact remains that the spread of the movement has been due to practical fruits, and the extremely practical turn of the American people has never been better shown than by the fact that this, their only decidedly original contribution to the systematic philosophy of life, should be intimately knit up with concrete therapeutics."[11]

When all was said and done, mind cure had performed the important task of reinterpreting the fundamental truths of religion in ways that made them palatable to unchurched Americans. James thought that its theories about the saving powers residing in the unconscious mind were "psychologically indistinguishable from Lutheran justification or Wesleyan acceptance."[12] Many persons unwilling to give themselves up to the wrathful God of Christianity were able to accept and assimilate psychological doctrines about inner-adjustment to invisible psychic powers. To these persons it was more important that their metaphysical assumptions square with empirical science than with religious orthodoxy. With what was more a personal plaudit than an objective description, James drew attention to the fact that "religion in the shape of mind-cure gives to some of us serenity, moral poise, and happiness, and prevents certain forms of disease as well as science does, or even better in a certain class of persons."[13]

Mesmerist psychology taught individuals how to connect themselves to an ultrarational sphere from whence saving energies flow. Like other modern theories it eschewed blind faith and, instead, asked persons to take better control over themselves and their environment; unlike other theories, it refused to restrict the world in which humans live to the one constructed by the five physical senses. In this sense, mesmerism voiced the middle-culture counterpart to the philosophical position which James designated as radical empiricism. A radical empiricism differs from scientific materialism in that it places no a priori constraints upon the kinds of data that reveal the true nature of reality. On the contrary, it is willing to find important hints concerning the deeper meaning of life in even the most-fleeting modes of experience.

> These deeper reaches are familiar to evangelical Christianity and to what is now-a-days becoming known as *"mind cure" religion* or *"new thought."* . . . There are *resources* in us that naturalism with its literal and legal virtues never recks of, possibilities that take our breath away, of *another kind of happiness and power,* based on giving up our own will and letting *something higher work for us,* and these seem to show a world wider than either physics or philistine ethics can imagine.[14]

James's prophetic eye erred only slightly when he predicted that mind cure psychology would play as great a part in the evolution of popular religion as had the Protestant Reformation.[15] True, mesmerism and its mind cure offspring petered out almost before James could get his laudatory estimation into print. But psychologized faiths have endured as a distinctive style of unchurched American religiosity. The glorification of untapped inner potentials has a powerful symbolic value to the Yankee spirit. Among other things, it reassures anxious souls of their convenantal relationship with God. By supplying a psychologically convincing explanation of "a communal ground of reality that is somehow the depth out of which our individuality arises," psychological movements such as mesmerism have rekindled commitment to notions of individual identity, personal freedom, and responsibility central to the Judeo-Christian tradition.[16] While such movements may appear offbeat to outsiders, their doctrines are strikingly supportive of the common core of beliefs which has shaped the American experience.[17]

Mesmerism did not disappear from the American scene because its theories about psychological healing were ineffectual or foolish. If that were the case, we wouldn't be witnessing the continued outcropping of very similar movements today. "Transpersonal" psychologies of one sort or another are almost universal features of human culture. The principal reason for this is that they undergird the ritual practices of those responsible for restoring individuals' ability to affirm what the larger community holds to be the ultimate source of moral values. What was unique about mesmerism's attempt to perform these curative functions was that it did so outside of any explicit ecclesiastical or theological context. The mesmerists foreswore Scripture, community tradition, and ethical reflection in their effort to reconcile men and women with the principle of spiritual creativity. Theirs was an unprecedented gambit to make psychology the bedrock of an all-encompassing orientation to life. Mesmerism's relatively brief tenure in American cultural life thus raises the important historical issue as to whether psychology, qua psychology, can provide an adequate basis for a normative healing system.

The mesmerists' early successes, we might recall, owed much to the period's revivalist metaphysical climate. The New England popular mind had become so familiar with the revivalists' practices that magnetic cures were readily understood to be but a curious permutation of well-known principles of spiritual renewal. The mesmerists, like the revivalists, made it possible for individuals to come into experiential contact with the nonmaterialistic forces that govern their lives. The mesmeric state of consciousness transmitted regenerative doses of what Victor Turner calls spontaneous or existential communitas. In other words, it temporarily displaced individuals from the mental and emotional stress of social existence so as to allow them to be inwardly connected with superhuman powers.[18] Poyen, Buchanan, Dods, Bush, and Sunderland, all understood their techniques to be putting men and women in touch with the true spiritual source of their being. Though most of these early mesmerists were aligned with theologically liberal Protestant sects, they never questioned the authoritative status of Christian doctrine. They were, without exception, convinced that magnetic cures strengthened Christian faith and quickened moral sensibility. Their writings fostered the identification of mesmeric renewal and progressive social reform. The mesmerizing process was described as restoring persons to their rightful role as active agents working for the unfoldment of God's preordained plans for creation. On the whole, mesmerism took root in this country as a ritual which unleashed religious enthusiasm for the purpose of sustaining, not supplanting, the normative cultural order formed by America's churches and the interdependence of community life.

Urbanization, industrialization, and the pluralization of intellectual authority—in short, the distinguishing characteristics of modernity—set mesmerism adrift from the Puritan-inspired assumptions about the norms of healthy human conduct. Quimby was the first to take notice of the growing chasm between the private and public spheres. He realized that Americans were no longer picking up a cohesive world view by simple osmosis. It was clear that most of his patients would never become fully functioning persons unless he drummed more-appropriate cognitive strategies into their heads. Quimby was convinced that certain ideas and beliefs had a definite correspondence to the superior powers garnered by the impressible state of consciousness. He told his patients these beliefs would help bring the potent forces of the unconscious mind into the service of their active personality. Quimby's successors went the further step of making "right beliefs" into a more or less complete description of how people ideally ought to think and act. The mind curists, by turning away from the actual practice of inner healing so as to give literary articulation to their psychologized philosophy of the good life, inadvertently severed the intrapsychic dimensions of personal growth from any necessary accommodation to those ideas and institutions which uphold moral community.

Ironically, not all of the mind curists were really all that interested in using mesmerist psychology as a means of becoming receptive to an unconscious "more." Spurred on by the appetites of a popular reading public, many of the mind cure authors became preoccupied with the tangible uses to which this "more" could be put. God became the All-supply who, via the psychic ethers, could manifest an objective condition to fulfill any and all subjective desires. God's spiritual energies were thought to be bound to a covenant of immutable psychological laws. Man's only obligation was to accurately phrase his demands through self-help formulae. Henry Wood put this sage counsel as well as any:

> Self-treatment or prayer is not a begging for special treatment, but rather a recognition that on the divine part everything already is perfect and that we only need conformity. It is simply a conscious taking of what already is provided. . . . Prayer is an effort toward realization in consciousness of what already is.[19]

Those following Wood's "simplified" version of New Thought needn't approach their spiritual source with prayerful humility or penitence; theirs was the spirit of "conscious taking." Little remained of the mystery and awe which surrounded the early discovery of the mesmeric state of consciousness. In Turner's terms, "spontaneous" communitas had gradually given way first to "normative" communitas and, finally, to "ideological" communitas. This movement reflected a decreasing concern with inner-transformation. Rather, the late New Thoughters or positive thinkers seemed more intent "to describe the external and visible effects—the outward form, it might be said—of an inward experience of existential communitas, and to spell out the optimal social conditions under which such experiences might be expected to flourish and multiply."[20] To many, the mesmerists' theories concerning the activation of the higher powers of the mind came to mean no more than a technique for projecting their own thoughts out onto the world of matter. They "entered the silence" for no other purpose than autosuggestion. Such a practice had the advantage of not introducing anything paranormal into the consciousness that might interfere with tenacious pursuit of success. The practice could even be conveniently sandwiched in during spare moments throughout the day. But whatever purposes it served, self-exploration certainly wasn't one of them. Never do we read of the later New Thought authors discovering something so radical about their spiritual selves that they are prompted to call their preselected "ideal suggestions" into question.

The mesmerists' metapsychology had originally been intended to shed light on human nature at what Bush called the "point where anthropology weds itself to theology." The mesmeric state of consciousness thus symbolized that phase of psychological awakening which discloses a dimension of "otherness" to our everyday sense of selfhood. It communicated the experienced conviction that each of us has a higher nature which is alone in harmony with God. Mesmerism made it perfectly clear that inner-fulfillment was man's rightful possession only to the degree that he learn to identify himself with this higher spiritual nature. But never were the paranormal features of the healing process taken as the defining characteristics of healthy human action. The value of the mesmeric state was thought to be sacramental only. It reassured persons that at one level, no matter how hidden from everyday awareness, they each participated in the divine nature of things. Beyond that the mesmerists had little to add—or delete—

from the prevailing consensus as to what God demanded of us in the way of responsible conduct.

The mesmerists' psychological description of human nature was intended to glorify men's inner potentials, not tell them how to build true community. When the mind curists inflated this psychological theory into a popular philosophy, they never expanded their thinking to fill this void. The consequence was a tragic one, as it encouraged persons to confuse intense preoccupation with their own inner being with the kind of lifestyle which would best serve them and their neighbors over the long run. The New Thought literature fairly addicted its readership to rhetoric describing a life free from impositions of any kind. It offered a convenient ideological shelter to many who were all too willing to be anesthetized to the burdensome demands life kept making on them. The cult of positive thinking lured them into pursuing a way of life which aimed to duplicate a mode of consciousness far removed from the give and take of social existence. This quest to make the ecstatic quality of the mesmeric state into a permanent mental abode almost perfectly exemplified Erik Erikson's observation that "even as the individual, in frantic search of his early hope-giving relationship, may end up lost in delusion and addiction, so are religions, when they lose their bonds with living ethics, apt to regress to the fostering of illusory and addictive promises or empty fantasy."[21]

The mind curists never fully came to terms with their world. All of their thinking about activating individuals' inner potentials took place in a timeless, spaceless, and society-less void. Their inattention to extrapersonal reality made it impossible for them to formulate a constructive theory of culture, a way of life or value system which, when internalized by society at large, works for the highest good of all.[22] If we define moral conduct as including only those actions which satisfy more rather than less human needs over the long run, then it is obvious that psychological healing necessarily entails helping clients take an ethical perspective on life. As Don Browning notes, the cure of souls is never simply "a matter of 'loosening people up,' helping them to become 'more open' or more 'spontaneous and flexible' . . . [it] must first be concerned to give a person a structure, a character, and an identity, a religio-cultural value system out of which to live . . . [it] must always include the incorporation of persons into a given moral universe."[23]

The mesmerists couldn't have been expected to order their clients to return to some small town where social sanctions insure harmony in the self-society relationship. Nor was it their prerogative to champion a particular philosophical or theological system as a monolithic source of moral vision. But their nonecclesiastical setting did not absolve them of their responsibility to make inner-healing the first step toward vibrant ethical existence. Their patients needed to be helped to function constructively in a society whose major institutions no longer socialized individuals into a self-consistent cultural pattern. However demanding it would have been to integrate ethical reflection into their healing system, the mesmerists' fatal error was that they never tried.

When Horatio Dresser proudly declared that "the New Thought is unquestionably the consciousness of individuality," he knew his words would appeal to the many suffocating under social pressures.[24] Doctrines about deeper levels of selfhood, mental atmospheres, and invisible thought vibrations invigorated downtrodden spirits by giving them new ways of acquiring a sense of self-worth. Unfortunately, they also fostered a notion of psychic causality, which made it appear that the only thing that really counted was how they thought about themselves. At the core of the New Thoughters' strategy for attaining the good life was the assumption that "all development is from an inner center or seed . . . the only cure comes through self-help, the only freedom through self-knowledge."[25] It was left to Henry Wood to put his finger on the practical upshot of a self-help religion. In his *The New Thought Simplified,* Wood pointed out that mind cure principles free us from dependence on others as we pursue self-advancement. The New Thought, he bragged, is "not generally organized as a church though it might not be inappropriate to call it the church of the Human Soul; its form of service is soulful aspiration, its sanctuary the spiritual consciousness, its temple the unseen, its social companions ideals, and its communion living contact with Universal spirit."[26]

It wasn't long before many woke up to the brute fact that ideals are lousy social companions. As an orientation to life, the New Thought philosophy aggravated rather than assuaged the emotional distance between people. Since the psychological model of human fulfillment New Thought borrowed from the mesmerists completely lacked any interpersonal variables, it couldn't demonstrate the strength-bestowing importance of such traditional virtues as cooperation, compromise, or delay of personal gratification. It did nothing to motivate individuals toward congregational life, deepening sensitivity and compassion, or breaking down self-imposed barriers to free and open communication. Thus, the nation's first popular psychology degenerated into an ideology that taught its adherents to systematically exclude the needs or opinions of others as illusory obstacles to self-actualization. The New Thought projected values which ironically prevented confused individuals from coming in touch with the most valuable healing resource of all—each other. Thus, it was more a symptom of than an antidote to modernity.

The mind curists never paused to ask whether the sense of inner-expansion was really an appropriate characterization of health. Their basic image of personal fulfillment was one of ecstasy and euphoric immediacy. Wholly lacking was the balancing idea that health also had to do with organizing human resources over a period of time. The New Thought literature encouraged its readers to abide in the psychic ethers to the point where they were no longer conscious of themselves as participants in the sequence of human generations. Institutional mechanisms are unnecessary in a world where thoughts are forces and all true development springs from within. But in the world of social experience, they alone link humans together in a responsible and caring way. The mind curists had no reason to found congregations—hence no Sunday Schools, adult interaction groups, or community action programs. Never did they concern themselves with transmitting skills and values at a person-to-person level.

The original impetus behind the mind cure movement had long been spent. Mesmerist psychology, which had earlier been so successful in uniting persons with a spiritual "more," lost its potency when no longer approached as a practical adjunct to one of several revival-oriented Protestant sects. All by itself it couldn't build the kind of personality traits which together generate a living community. Since it had no real recruiting mechanisms and certainly no institutionalized means for bringing up a second generation of mind cure students, its social constituency finally became too limited to survive.

There was, then, something inherently counterproductive in the mind curists' attempt to supply unchurched Americans with a spiritual philosophy of life. Interestingly, the problem wasn't that mesmerist psychology was an inappropriate vehicle for religious revitalization. As both a ritualized experience and a symbolic theory of inner-healing, it had turned Americans beyond materialistic sources of identification and taught them to align themselves with an immanent divinity. What eventually made the mind curists' ideas become so ephemeral was that they failed to subordinate psychological insights about human nature to a larger set of religiocultural understandings. Mesmerism's psychological interpretation of spiritual fulfillment was never supplemented by any broader inquiry into the objective requirements of a nurturing culture. Nothing in its monocausal analysis of spiritual health forced its adherents to arrange their personal energies into a hierarchy of moral obligations.[27] Nor did it ever insist that they learn to forego certain desires in favor of cultivating ones that would strengthen themselves and others over the long run. As a consequence, mind cure's healing message was pathetically anemic when it came to offering practical guidance to persons suffering from a society whose institutions were already too diffuse to force them out of narcissism and social passivity. Preoccupied with their own psychological depths, the mind curists became permanently encapsulated from the surrounding and intermediary powers through which we are able to satisfy one another's needs.

The mesmerists had ushered in a new era in the American cure of souls. They were the first to popularize psychological ideas as a resource for religious self-understanding. In an age in which many hungered for nontraditional sources of spiritual edification, they helped make human consciousness itself a medium through which to glimpse the divine. It appears, however, that the mesmerists' psychological doctrines were in many respects solipsistic: they failed to take into account the moral values and institutional structures which alone link subjective vitality with responsible social conduct. Mesmerism had entered into American cultural thought as an innovative extension of revivalist religiosity. When its theories lost overt identification with this moral and metaphysical context, it lost its transformative power. America's first nonecclesiastical practice of spiritual healing ultimately showed itself to be little more than an interesting detour. Its theories fell harmlessly by the wayside as modern men and women continued to search for ways of reconciling themselves, not only with higher spiritual powers, but also with one another.

Notes

Foreword

1. Max Weber, *The Protestant Ethic and the Spirit of Capitalism* (New York: Charles Scribner's Sons, 1958), pp. 111–128. Richard Baxter's *Christian Directory*, a manual for the theological guidance of individuals concerned over the matter of their election, is the crucial datum upon which Weber built his thesis concerning the origin and cultural consequences of the Protestant ethic.

2. Frederick J. Streng, *Understanding Religious Man* (Encino: Dickensen Publishing Company, 1976), p. 6.

3. See William Clebsch's and Charles Jaekle's *Pastoral Care in Historical Perspective* (New York: Jason Aronson, 1975). Their discussion of the cure of souls, which they define as "helping . . . acts directed toward healing, sustaining, guiding, and reconciling of troubled persons whose troubles arise in the contexts of ultimate meanings and concerns" (p. 4), furnishes criteria which will guide our interpretation of mesmerism's role in the unchurched practice of spiritual care and guidance.

4. Ibid., p. 5.

5. Though historical rather than constructive in nature, one concern of this book is to demonstrate the important sense in which these materials and the kinds of judgments to which they give rise are germane to a critical analysis of our "psychological society." I might direct the interested reader to such seminal studies as Don Browning's *The Moral Context of Pastoral Care* (Phil-

adelphia: Westminster Press, 1976), Martin Gross's *The Psychological Society* (New York: Random House, 1978), Russell Jacoby's *Social Amnesia* (Boston: Beacon Press, 1975), Christopher Lasch's *The Culture of Narcissism* (New York: W. W. Norton, 1979), and Phillip Rieff's *Triumph of the Therapeutic* (New York: Harper and Row, 1966).

Chapter 1

1. There are a number of excellent studies of Mesmer and his healing science. Unfortunately, only a few are in English. The best of these is to be found in the opening chapters of Henri Ellenberger's *The Discovery of the Unconscious* (New York: Basic Books, 1970). Others include: Vincent Buranelli's *Franz Anton Mesmer: The Wizard from Vienna* (New York: McCann, Cowan, and Geoghegan, 1975); Margaret Goldsmith's *Franz Anton Mesmer: The History of an Idea* (London: Barkert, 1934); and Frank Podmore's *From Mesmer to Christian Science* (New York: University Books, 1963).

2. A succinct account of the cultural context in which Mesmer formulated his twenty-seven principles can be found in Ellenberger's *Discovery of the Unconscious.*

3. A complete English translation of these twenty-seven principles can be found in Goldsmith, *Franz Anton Mesmer.* The following translation is, however, my own.

4. A reasonably coherent summary of the investigations performed by the two French commissions is to be found in Podmore, *From Mesmer to Christian Science.* I might forewarn the interested reader that Podmore, an active member of the Society for Psychical Research, imposes his own ideological blinders upon the material. Convinced that thought transference is the prime reality behind the occult and supernatural, Podmore does not encourage his readers to take alternative explanations seriously.

5. Podmore, *From Mesmer to Christian Science,* p. 59.

6. Robert Darnton, *Mesmerism and the End of the Enlightenment in France* (New York: Schocken Books, 1970), p. vii.

7. Ibid., p. 161.

8. Podmore, *From Mesmer to Christian Science,* p. 78.

9. John Esdaile, an English physician, is widely acknowledged for having made pioneering contributions in the development of anesthesiology with the benefit of hypnotism (although Esdaile understood himself to be using mesmerism—a belief which later medical historians have felt it necessary to correct by substituting the more acceptable term *hypnosis*). A 1957 review of Esdaile's work makes the revealing observation that *"in spite of* Esdaile's belief in 'thought transference' or clairvoyance, his logical deductions and classic description of mesmeric anesthesia are scientifically valid today" (William S. Kroger, *Hypnosis in Medicine and Surgery* [New York: Julian Press, 1957], p. viii; italics mine).

10. Henri Ellenberger's account of the history and evolution of dynamic psychiatry from Mesmer through Freud in *Discovery of the Unconscious* is, to my knowledge, unexcelled.

11. The alleged incidence of telepathy during hypnosis and intensely empathetic psychotherapy is a subject that continues to find strong advocates. The interested reader might consult J. Eisenbud's *PSI and Psychoanalysis* (New York: Grune and Stratton, 1957); J. Ehrenwald's *The ESP Experience* (New York: Basic Books, 1978); or any of several studies of Sigmund Freud's ambivalent stance on this matter, with Chapter IV of Reuben Rainey's *Freud as a Student of Religion* (Missoula: Scholar Press, 1975) being a good starting point.

12. This statement is in need of some qualification. Ellenberger (p. 159) reminds us that Schelling, Fichte, and Schopenhauer were each intrigued by the ways in which mesmerism contributed to an experimental metaphysics. In addition, both Darnton and Podmore provide short discussions of mesmerism's affinity with occult religious movements in both France and Germany. My point here is merely that we would be hard pressed to argue that mesmerism exerted anywhere near the kind of shaping influence in European religious life that it did with the so-called harmonial religions which have dotted the American religious scene for well over a century.

Chapter 2

1. The entire letter of May 14, 1784 is included as an appendix to J. P. F. Deleuze's *Practical Instructions in Animal Magnetism,* 2d ed. (New York: Samuel Wells, 1879).

2. Poyen gives a personal account of his efforts in his *Progress of Animal Magnetism in New England* (Boston: Weeks, Jordan, and Co., 1837). Two other resources are useful for reconstructing Poyen's early role in the dissemination of mesmerism in America: Margaret Goldsmith's *Franz Anton Mesmer* and an 1843 pamphlet entitled *The History and Philosophy of Animal Magnetism with Practical Instructions for the Exercise of Its Power* (written and published in Boston under the pseudonym, "A Practical Magnetizer").

3. Poyen cataloged the "phenomena of magnetic Somnambules" as follows: "(1) Suspension, more or less complete, of the external sensibility; (2) intimate connexion with the magnetizer and with no other one; (3) influence of the will; (4) communication of thought; (5) clairvoyance, or the faculty of seeing through various parts of the body, the eyes remaining closed; (6) unusual development of sympathy, of memory, and of the power of imagination; (7) faculty for sensing the symptoms of diseases and prescribing proper remedies for them; (8) entire forgetting, after awakening, of what had transpired during the state of somnambulism" (*Progress,* p. 63).

4. Poyen, *Progress,* p. 35. The reader might wish to consult the *Boston Courier,* January 6, 1837, for a representative account of Poyen's impact on New England audiences.

5. William Stone, *Letter to Dr. A. Brigham on Animal Magnetism* (New York: George Dearborn and Co., 1837), p. 81.

6. Poyen, *Progress,* p. 55.

7. Ibid., p. 27.

8. Ibid., p. 88 (italics mine).

9. Ibid.

10. William Stone, *Letter to Dr. Brigham.*

11. Readers interested in literature describing "out of the body experiences" might wish to examine Stone's description (ibid., pp. 15–49) of a mesmerically anesthetized patient who,

with eyes bandaged, was said to have recounted events occurring in various parts of the room during the course of his operation.

12. Charles Durant, *Exposition, or a New Theory of Animal Magnetism* (New York: Wiley and Putnam, 1837).

13. Charles Poyen, *A Letter to Col. William Stone of New York* (Boston: Weeks, Jordan, and Co., 1837).

14. Poyen was not alone in his public assault on Durant's integrity. Similar ad hominem rebuttals of Durant's allegations are to be found in LaRoy Sunderland's *"Confessions of a Magnetizer" Exposed* (Boston: Redding and Co., 1845) and *The Philosophy of Animal Magnetism, Together with the System of Manipulating Adopted to Produce Ecstasy and Somnambulism* (Philadelphia: Merrihew and Gunn, 1837) issued under the pseudonym "A Gentleman of Philadelphia."

15. Poyen, *Letter to Stone,* p. 45.

16. Robert Collyer, *Lights and Shadows of American Life* (Boston: Brainard and Co., 1838).

17. Robert Collyer, *The Manual of Phrenology* (Dayton: B. F. Ellis, 1838). While written prior to his interest in mesmerism, this book is of interest to this study in that it typifies phrenological writings circulating in America during this period.

18. Collyer, *Lights and Shadows,* pp. 7, 11.

19. A Practical Magnetizer, *History,* p. 8.

20. Ibid., p. 9.

21. A Gentleman of Philadelphia, *Philosophy of Animal Magnetism.*

22. Included in one list of twenty-five American magnetizers were four ministers, five professors, and several medical physicians. See Chapter Two of A Practical Magnetizer's *History.*

23. From an unsigned article in *Buchanan's Journal of Man* 1 (1849): 319. Buchanan's journal was published in Cincinnati by Shepard and Morgan.

24. Ibid. (italics mine).

25. Anonymous, *Confessions of a Magnetizer, Being an Expose of Animal Magnetism* (Boston: Gleason Publishing Hall, 1845), p. 2.

26. David M. Reese, *Humbugs of New York* (New York: John Taylor, 1838), pp. 35ff.

27. Anonymous, *Confessions of a Magnetizer*. It is doubtful that the author had a very deep grasp of mesmerism or the techniques for inducing a profound state of consciousness in his subjects. His accounts amount to little more than stories of simple stage hypnosis and, when coupled with several factual inaccuracies in his theoretical discussion, would seem to indicate that his interpretations are unreliable.

28. From an 1837 entry in *The Journals and Miscellaneous Notebooks of Ralph Waldo Emerson* (Cambridge, Mass.: Belknap Press, 1965), 5: 388.

29. Ibid.

30. Nathaniel Hawthorne, *The American Notebook* (New Haven: Yale University Press, 1932), p. 93.

31. Nathaniel Hawthorne, in a letter written from Brook Farm on October 18, 1841.

32. Nathaniel Hawthorne, *The Blithedale Romance* (Columbus: Ohio State University Press, 1964), p. 198.

33. Edgar Allen Poe, *Collected Works,* 3 vols. (Cambridge, Mass.: Harvard University Press, 1978), 3:1029.

34. Ibid., 3:1243.

35. Elizabeth Barrett Browning in a letter cited in Mary Phillip's *Edgar Allen Poe, The Man* (Chicago: Winston and Co., 1926), p. 1075. Another valuable study of Poe's interest in mesmerism is John H. Ingram's *Edgar Allen Poe* (London: Hogg and Row, 1880).

36. Many American mesmerists downplayed their overt connections with the movement in order to avoid being dismissed as lunatics or charlatans. Many did so by relabeling their theory so as to clearly distinguish themselves from mesmerism's more banal elements. Of major consequence was the effort by early New Thoughters such as Horatio Dresser and Warren Felt Evans to all but obscure the mesmerist foundations of their healing practices. Dresser and others were so concerned to defend Mind Cure/New Thought's reputation that they deliberately misrepresented the history and techniques of their healing practice so as not to conjure up negative sentiments toward their mesmerist-based theories. We will give closer attention to mesmerism's de-

velopment into Mind Cure in Chapters 5 and 6. The New Thoughters' position was made all the more precarious by Mary Baker Eddy's diatribe against her former mentor (Quimby), whom she accused of being a "mere mesmerist" and, thus, bereft of loftier Christian insights. She also accused her detractors of practicing "malicious animal magnetism" against her and her followers.

37. Sunderland, *Confessions*, p. 22.

38. A Practical Magnetizer, *History*, p. 15.

39. As recent as 1907, Dr. Weston Bayley was arguing that the terms *hypnotism* and *mesmerism* were by no means interchangeable. The latter, he contended, pertains to a much deeper psychic reality in which the subject comes under the influence of a transpersonal energy (animal magnetism) undetected at other levels of consciousness. Weston Bayley, "Some Facts in Mesmerism," *Proceedings of the American Society for Psychical Research* 1(1907): 8–22.

40. Townshend's phenomenological typology of human consciousness became the psychological model upon which later writers, up to and including the New Thought authors of the 1870s and 80s, elaborated philosophical systems connecting man's inner life with a wider spiritual environment.

41. The following descriptions represent a distillation of the virtually identical typologies found in Townshend, Haddock, Dods, Sunderland, Caldwell, Buchanan, and A Practical Magnetizer. This intertextual consistency is, in part, attributable to their familiarity with one another's writings. Yet each author carefully describes the experimental findings which led to his own categorizations. It is interesting, in this light, to note that recent research by experimental psychologists suggests that various altered states of consciousness, such as hypnosis, dreaming, drug-induced states, etc., all have their own unique ("state-bound") properties and structural characteristics. See, for instance, Charles Tart's *States of Consciousness* (New York: E. P. Dutton, 1975).

42. Reverend Chauncy Townshend, *Facts in Mesmerism* (London: Bailliere Press, 1844), p. 222.

43. It would be a gross miscarriage of historical justice to dismiss the many reported cases of mesmeric cure as either outright fraud or simple coincidence. Whether these cures pertained to organic (physical/material) or functional (psychosomatic) ailments is, of course, another matter. George Sandby might supply us with a partial hint in his analysis of mesmerism's remarkable ability to cure deafness and blindness. He reported that "the benefit has been obtained by degrees; and in no instance has a cure been produced where the privation has arisen from a structural defect commencing with birth." *Mesmerism and Its Opponents* (London: Longren, Brown, Green, 1844), p. 217.

44. Typical accounts of mesmerism's curative feats are to be found in the previously cited works by Poyen, Sunderland, Townshend, and Sandby and in Hartshorne's appendix to his translation of Deleuze's work.

45. Both Townshend and John Dods (see Chapter 4) purport to have used their power of animal magnetism to restore eyesight to the blind. The account of Mesmer's treatment of blindness in the case of Maria-Theresia Paradis makes for interesting reading (see Ellenberger, *Discovery*, pp. 60–61).

46. Joseph Buchanan, *Neurological System of Anthropology* (Cincinnati, 1854), p. 252.

47. Ibid., p. 253. The belief that select individuals could exercise the entrancing and curative properties of animal magnetism over large distances—with the obvious implication that mesmerism was not simply a psychological system in the usual sense of that term—persisted from the accounts of Mesmer's own practices up to and including those of Phineas P. Quimby's.

48. Ibid.

49. The typologies employed by American mesmerists bear a striking resemblance to the one which a German mesmerist, Carl Kluge, put in his 1811 textbook on animal magnetism. Kluge, too, divided the magnetic state into six states or degrees. He notes that very few subjects are able to reach the last three stages, particularly the sixth one, which he believed held the highest importance for scientific and philosophical researchers. Although A Practical Magnetizer cited Kluge in his 1841 pam-

phlet, there is no evidence to suggest that the American mesmerists consciously borrowed from Kluge's findings. His six degrees (see Ellenberger, *Discovery,* p. 78) were:"(1) waking state, with a sensation of increased warmth (2) half-sleep (3) 'inner darkness,': that is, sleep proper and insensitivity (4) 'inner clarity,': that is, heightened consciousness of one's body, extrasensory perception (5) 'self-contemplation': The subject's ability to perceive with great clarity the interior of his own body and those of whom he is put into rapport [i.e., clairvoyant diagnosis] (6) 'universal clarity': the removal of veils of time and space and the subject perceives things hidden in the past, the future, or at remote distances."

Chapter 3

1. The best account of phrenology's short tenure in American intellectual circles is John Davies's *Phrenology: Fact and Science* (New Haven: Yale University Press, 1955).

2. Reese, *Humbugs of New York,* p. 86.

3. From LaRoy Sunderland's periodical *The Magnet* (1841), as cited by Davies, *Phrenology,* p. 126.

4. Researchers interested in the personality traits associated with ease of entrance into altered states of consciousness might be interested in Buchanan's comment that "impressibility lies in a group of organs which sustain it, and may be expected to accompany its development. Sensibility, somnalence, dreaming, ideality, modesty, humility, disease, relaxation . . . religious excitement, sympathy, sincerity, love, thoughtfulness, philanthropy . . . in short all amiable, sensitive, intellectual, refining, relaxing influences are promative of impressibility" (Buchanan, *Neurological System of Anthropology* [Cincinnati: n.p., 1854], p. 40).

5. Joseph Buchanan, *Buchanan's Journal of Man* 1 (1849): 419.

6. J. Stanley Grimes, *The Mysteries of the Head and Heart Explained,* 3d ed. (Chicago: Sumner and Co., 1881), p. 251.

7. From an unsigned article in *Buchanan's Journal of Man* 1 (1849): 319.

8. Poyen, *Letter to Stone,* p. 27.

9. Sunderland, *Confessions,* pp. 19–22.

10. Grimes, *Mysteries.*

11. William Carpenter, *Mesmerism and Spiritualism: Historically and Scientifically Considered* (New York: D. Appleton and Co., 1889).

12. John Bovee Dods, *The Philosophy of Mesmerism* (Boston: William Hall, 1843).

13. The reference here is to the 1837 pamphlet issued by A Gentlemen of Philadelphia.

14. Sunderland, *Pathetism* (Boston: White and Potter, 1847). Sunderland's discussion of the right and left brains and his references to "two alternating forces of life" are especially interesting with reference to contemporary theories of the bihemispherical structure of the brain.

15. A Gentlemen of Philadelphia, *Philosophy.*

16. *Library of Mesmerism and Psychology* (New York: Fowler and Wells, 1852).

17. Townshend, *Facts,* p. 273.

18. J. Stanley Grimes, *Etherology and the Phreno-philosophy of Mesmerism and Magic Eloquence: Including a New Philosophy of Sleep and of Consciousness* (Boston: James Munroe and Co., 1850), p. 18.

19. For the most part unchurched, Caldwell's religious sympathies clearly lay with progressive-minded groups such as the Unitarians, whose liberal views he publicly supported in a local dispute with Baptist and Presbyterian clergy.

20. Charles Caldwell, "Thoughts on the True Connexion of Phrenology and Religion," *American Phrenological Journal* 1 (1839).

21. Ibid., p. 12.

22. Charles Caldwell, *Facts in Mesmerism and Thoughts on Its Causes and Uses* (Louisville: Prentice and Weissinger, 1842), p. 3.

23. Ibid., p. 124.

24. Ibid., p. 14.

25. Ibid., p. 61.

26. Not incidentally, Buchanan eventually moved to California where he become interested in spiritualism—himself becoming a medium for the discarnate spirit of "St. John."

27. Joseph Buchanan, *Neurological System of Anthropology* (Cincinnati: n.p., 1854), p. 195.

28. Ibid., Appendix I.
29. Ibid.
30. Ibid.
31. Ibid.
32. John Bovee Dods, *The Philosophy of Electrical Psychology* (New York: Fowler and Wells, 1850), p. 36.
33. Townshend, *Facts*, p. 370.
34. A Gentlemen of Philadelphia, *Philosophy*, p. 68.
35. Dods, *Electrical Psychology*, p. 36.

Chapter 4

1. Collyer's *Mesmeric Magazine* was abandaned after its very first issue. *The Journal of the Phreno-Magnetic Society of Cincinnati* also managed but one offering. Slightly more successful was Sunderland's *The Magnet*, which remained intact for nearly two years. Sunderland's relative success was at least partially due to the fact that his editorial policies were so eclectic as to exclude almost no one from his readership. The journal's subtitle read "dedicated to the investigation of human physiology, embracing vitality, pathetism, psychology, phrenopathy, phrenology, neurology, physiognomy and magnetism." The list is important in at least one respect. It shows that early psychological theorists weren't altogether sure just what it was they were talking about.
2. *Confessions of a Magnetizer*, p. 13.
3. Dods, *Mesmerism*, p. 1.
4. Dods, *Electrical Psychology*, p. 9.
5. Dods, *Mesmerism*, p. 3.
6. Joseph Haddock, *Somnalism and Psycheism or the Science of the Soul as Revealed by Mesmerism* (London: Hodson, 1848), p. 4.
7. Theodore Léger, *Animal Magnetism, or Psychodunamy* (New York: D. Appleton, 1846).
8. See Arnold van Gennep's *The Rites of Passage* (London: Routledge and Kegan Paul, 1909).
9. From the French mesmerist Deleuze's *Practical Instructions in Animal Magnetism* which, in its English translation, served as one of the American mesmerists' basic instruction manuals.
10. Buchanan, *Neurological Anthropology*, p. 257.
11. A Practical Magnetizer, *History*, p. 19.

12. Dods, *Electrical Psychology*, p. 57.

13. Perry Miller, *Errand Into the Wilderness* (Cambridge, Mass.: Belknap Press, 1975), p. 55.

14. Ibid., p. 71.

15. Charles G. Finney, cited in William McLoughlin's *Revivals, Awakenings, and Reform* (Chicago: University of Chicago Press, 1978), p. 125.

16. Charles G. Finney, cited in William McLoughlin's *Modern Revivalism* (New York: Ronald Press, 1959), p. 84.

17. Ibid.

18. Charles G. Finney, cited in McLoughlin's *Revivals*, p. 126.

19. Whitney R. Cross, *The Burned-Over District* (Ithaca: Cornell University Press, 1950), p. 183.

20. Ibid.

21. Ibid., p. 175. The quoted material comes from a 17 November 1830 communication from William Clark, Cooperstown, to Charles Finney.

22. Dods, *Electrical Psychology*, p. 16.

23. Whitney Cross demonstrates this connection between revivalist religiosity and mesmerist psychology: see Cross, *Burned-Over District*, pp. 275, 326.

24. Robert Baird, *Religion in American* (New York: Harper and Brothers, 1844), p. 583.

25. Herbert Hovenkamp's *Science and Religion in America, 1800–1860* (Philadelphia: University of Pennsylvania Press, 1978) is a competent guide to antebellum theological uses of science.

26. Cross, *Burned-Over District*, p. 342.

27. J. Stanley Grimes in a volume coauthored with John Dods, *Electrical Psychology* (London: Griffin and Company, 1851), p. 145.

28. Theodore Léger, *Animal Magnetism, or Psychodunamy* (New York: S. Appleton, 1846), p. 18.

29. William Clebsch, *American Religious Thought* (Chicago: The University of Chicago Press, 1973), p. xvi. I understand this religious posture, which is shared by such otherwise unlikely company as Jonathan Edwards, Ralph Waldo Emerson, and William James, to be similar to what Sydney Ahlstrom designates harmo-

nial religion. Ahlstrom defines this perduring strand of American religiosity as "those forms of piety and belief in which spiritual composure, physical health and even economic well-being are understood to flow from a person's rapport with the cosmos." From his *A Religious History of the American People* (New York: Image Books, 1975), 2: 528.

30. John Dods, *Thirty Short Sermons, Both Doctrinal and Practical* (Boston: Whittemore, 1842).

31. Ibid., p. 114.

32. Ibid., p. 82.

33. Ibid., p. 320.

34. Whitney Cross has noted that "the religious radicals also continued to be mainly one-idea men. Many of them turned about with amazing speed and frequency after 1837, but at any given moment they stuck to one cause and believed that to be the single panacea for the ills of their age . . . a large number, to be sure, transferred their fervor to newly current fads of European origin: mesmerism, phrenology, Swedenborgianism, or Fourierism" (*Burned-Over District*, p. 275).

35. Dods, *Electrical Psychology,* p. 22.

36. Dods, *Mesmerism,* p. 137.

37. Dods, *Electrical Psychology,* p. 28.

38. Ibid., p. 223.

39. Ibid., Lecture VI, "Existence of Deity Proved from Nation."

40. Ibid., p. 92.

41. Ibid., p. 71.

42. Ibid., Lecture IV, "Philosophy of Disease and Nervous Forces."

43. Ibid., p. 223.

44. Ibid., p. 158.

45. Ibid., p. 251.

46. Ibid.

47. John Bovee Dods, *Spirit Manifestations: Examined and Explained* (New York: De Witt and Davenport, 1854), p. 81. The American mesmerists were generally concerned with subordinating psychological understandings to the authority of the Bible.

Mesmerism was believed to be demonstrating biblical passages, not supplanting them. George Sandby's *Mesmerism and Its Opponents* (London: Longren, Brown, and Green, 1844), pp. 226–263, gives an extended discussion of mesmerism's relationship to biblical religion.

48. Ibid., p. 110.

49. An especially concise account of "the Swedenborgism impulse" can be found in Sydney Ahlstrom's *A Religious History of the American People* (New Haven: Yale University Press, 1972), pp. 483–488.

50. John Humphrey Noyes, cited in Cross, *Burned-Over District,* p. 343.

51. An excellent discussion of Swedenborg's influence upon Emerson is to be found in Kenneth W. Cameron's *Young Emerson's Transcendental Vision* (Hartford: Transcendental Books, 1971). Quotation from p. 297.

52. Cited in ibid., p. 297.

53. Baird, *Religion in America,* p. 567.

54. Ibid.

55. George Bush, *Mesmer and Swedenborg* (New York: John Allen, 1847), p. 69.

56. Ibid., p. 147.

57. Ibid., p. 15.

58. Ibid., p. 160.

59. Ibid., p. 137.

60. Ibid., p. xii.

61. R. Laurence Moore, *In Search of White Crows* (New York: Oxford University Press, 1977), p. 7.

62. Thomas Lake Harris, quoted in ibid., p. 12.

63. Thomas Lake Harris, quoted in ibid., p. 18.

64. Andrew Jackson Davis, *The Magic Staff* (New York: J. S. Brown, 1857). See also the chapter entitled "My Early Experiences" in Davis's *The Great Harmonia* (Boston: Mussey and Co., 1852).

65. Davis, *Harmonia,* p. 26.

66. Ibid., p. 31.

67. Ibid., p. 45. Historian Henri Ellenberger *(Discovery)* has

advanced a hypothesis concerning the instrumental role of what he calls "creative illness" in the discovery of psychological insights. It is interesting in this light to note that, just prior to his "breakthrough," Davis underwent a severe emotional breakdown. While the details are unclear, he is believed to have been unconscious for well over a day. He later claimed to have been "living wholly in the interior world." It was from this point onward that his journeys into the magnetic state would be imbued with great spiritual significance.

68. Davis, *Harmonia*, p. 47.

69. The reader might remember that Poe's "Mesmeric Revelations" was based upon his firsthand observation of Davis's mesmeric séances. Poe later remarked that surely there couldn't be more things in heaven and earth than are dreamed of in Andrew Jackson Davis's philosophy.

70. Bush, *Mesmer*, p. 171.

71. R. Laurence Moore *(In Search)* has written a perceptive criticism of American spiritualism precisely on these grounds.

72. It might be pointed out that several decades later Madame Blavatsky and Colonel Henry Olcott cited mesmerism as congenial with Theosophical teachings. Blavatsky's *Isis Unveiled* (London: The Theosophical Society, 1877) contains a long and much-detailed treatment of the subject. It is importent to note that she made a distinction between two kinds of magnetization: the "purely animal" and the "transcendent [which depends] on the will and knowledge of the mesmerizer, as well as on the degree of spirituality of the subject" (p. 178).

73. Cross, *Burned-Over District*, p. 342.

74. McLoughlin, *Revivals*, p. 2.

75. Ibid.

76. Ibid., p. 103.

77. Haddock, *Somnalism and Psycheism*, p. x.

78. One of the mesmerists' prime goals was to offer "rational" explanations of religious beliefs and practices. For example, Dods thought himself to be making Jesus' healing ministry more palatable to the modern mind when he drew attention to the fact that "it is undeniably true that there was always something

passed from our Savior, when he exercised the gift of healing" (Dods, *Mesmerism,* p. 75). Several mesmerists proposed that their doctrines fully accounted for such religious phenomena as Whitefield's revivals, spiritualism, Joseph Smith's revelations, and the Salem witchcraft incidents. Though it stands alone in the mesmerists' literature, Grimes's bold assertion that modern man "is forced to adapt the literal meaning of the Bible to the teachings of modern science" (*Problems of Creation* [Chicago: Sumner and Co., 1881], p. 41) shows the direction to which the mesmerists' empirical learnings pointed.

79. Dods, *Mesmerism.*
80. Townshend, *Facts,* p. 360.

Chapter 5

1. The selection of 1860 and 1885 is intended to give rough chronological reference to three successive phases in mesmerism's journey through the American popular mind. Between 1835 and 1860 mesmerism was principally a healing ritual that focused upon transmitting animal magnetism from operator to patient. Although the early American mesmerists recognized the importance of the mesmeric state for a normative philosophy of life, they did little to show individuals just what changes in their self-understanding were called for. The second period, extending from 1860 to 1885, covers the life and work of Phineas P. Quimby and his disciples. Together they transformed mesmerism's doctrines into a philosophy of systematic inner-adjustment. Mesmerist psychology here became a conceptual paradigm or nucleus for their self-help guide to physical, mental, and spiritual fulfillment. Between 1885 and 1900 mesmerism's theory of subconscious mental energies was further attenuated into programs of positive thinking—thus constituting a third period in mesmerism's interaction with American culture.

2. James J. King, "The Present Condition of New York City Above Fourteenth Street, 1888," in Robert D. Cross, ed., *The Church and the City* (Indianapolis: Bobbs-Merrill, 1967), p. 30.

3. Ibid.

4. Robert Wiebe, *The Search for Order* (New York: Hill and Wang, 1967), p. 4.

5. Ibid., pp. xii, 12.

6. John Lancaster Spalding, "The Country and the City, 1880," in Cross, *Church and City*, pp. 3–28.

7. Ahlstrom, *A Religious History*, p. 736.

8. Washington Gladden, "The Fratricide of the Churches," in Cross, *Church and City*, pp. 40–55.

9. Victor Turner, *The Ritual Process* (Ithaca: Cornell University Press, 1977), p. 97.

10. George Beard, *American Nervousness* (New York: G. P. Putnam, 1881).

11. Ibid., p. 99.

12. Arthur Schlesinger, "A Critical Period in American Religion, 1875–1900," *Proceedings of the Massachusetts Historical Society* 64 (1930–1932): 523–538.

13. Anthony Wallace, *Religion: An Anthropological Study* (New York: Random House, 1966), p. 156.

14. Ibid.

15. McLoughlin, *Revivals*, p. 2.

16. Ibid., p. xiii.

17. The fact that the counseling setting can profoundly influence the development of a theological tradition has been soundly established by Max Weber in his studies of the Protestant ethic and his work on the religions of both India and China. Following Weber's lead, it is interesting to speculate as to what role American psychologies have played in the development of such normative intellectual disciplines as philosophy and theology. I might make the initial observation that not only can mesmerism be considered a legitimate precursor to the Third Great Awakening, but it could also be argued that many of the so-called humanistic psychologies that emerged in the late 1950s anticipated what McLoughlin labels the "Fourth Great Awakening, 1960–90." See his *Revivals*, Chapter Six.

18. Wallace enumerates five distinct phases, or psychological mechanisms, which he feels comprise rituals of revitalization. Each can be argued to have been operative in the Mind Cure or New Thought program: (1) pre-learning (through dissemination of Mind Cure ideas in literature; magazine articles, and lectures); (2) separation (performed psychologically by inducing a mes-

meric state of consciousness and sociologically through the act of joining a group and acquiring the identity of a group member); (3) suggestion (made particularly effective through daily meditational/mesmerizing exercises and techniques geared to program the subconscious mind with positive affirmations); (4) execution (encouraged in the form of daily mental exercises and in the systematic cultivation of positive thinking); and (5) maintenance (helping members to sustain their newly acquired identities through the formation of local clubs or societies and the distribution of periodical literature). The fact that Quimby and his followers introduced changes into mesmerist psychology which successfully institutionalized these ritualistic processes enabled their healing-based philosophy to serve as a therapeutic foil to the social strain and mental dis-ease accompanying the onset of modernity.

19. Quimby's life and works have received attention in a number of works dealing with the New Thought movement; however, none are to be fully trusted due to their misplaced reliance on Horatio Dresser's editorial commentary in his edition of *The Quimby Manuscripts* (New York: Thomas Crowell, 1921). Dresser was so concerned with exonerating Quimby from Mary Baker Eddy's charge that he had been a "mere mesmerist" that he all but obscured the paramount role that mesmerist metapsychology had in the early development of the Mind Cure or New Thought philosophy. Duly forewarned, the reader might refer to Charles Braden's *Spirits in Rebellion* (Dallas: Southern Methodist University Press, 1963), Horatio Dresser's *Health and the Inner Life: An Account of the Life and Teachings of P. P. Quimby* (New York: G. P. Putnam's Sons, 1906), or the relevant sections of Robert Peel's *Mary Baker Eddy: The Years of Discovery* (New York: Holt, Rinehart and Winston, 1966).

20. Quimby, *Manuscripts,* p. 30.

21. Ibid.

22. Ibid., p. 180.

23. Ibid.

24. Ibid., p. 194.

25. Ibid., p. 319.

26. Peel, *Mary Baker Eddy*, p. 154.

27. Ibid., pp. 154–165. The reader will note that Peel, an apologist for Christian Science, attempts to credit Mrs. Eddy with originality by minimizing Quimby's attention to the educative/religious dimensions of Mind Cure. Peel's error is, in this respect, the counterpart of Horatio Dresser's likewise ideologically biased interpretation of Quimby's practice.

28. It is interesting to note the close resemblance of Quimby's healing methods to those described by Lawrence LeShan in his *The Medium, the Mystic, and the Physicist* (New York: Viking Press, 1974). LeShan describes two quite distinct modes of psychic healing—both of which were employed by Quimby on different occasions. In "Type I" healing, "the healer goes into an altered state of consciousness in which he views himself and the healee as one entity. . . . [This establishes] a moment of such intense knowledge of the Clairvoyant Reality structure of the cosmos that it filled [the patient's] consciousness entirely, so that there was—for that moment—nothing else in the field of knowing to prevent the healing results from occurring." In "Type II" healing cure depends upon a "flow of energy" or the transmission of psychic energy into the affected body organ (pp. 107, 112).

29. Quimby, *Manuscripts*, p. 76. Quimby's descriptions of the "mental atmospheres" fostered an informal alliance between mesmerism and sundry occult groups investigating such metaphysical conceptions as the "astral body" or "aura."

30. Ibid., p. 82.

31. Cited in Peel, *Mary Baker Eddy*, p. 155.

32. Ibid., p. 157.

33. Quimby, *Manuscripts*, p. 52.

34. Ibid., p. 342.

35. Quoted in Peel, *Mary Baker Eddy*, p. 165.

36. Ibid., p. 399.

37. Quoted in Braden, *Spirits*, p. 63.

38. Erik Erikson, *Insight and Responsibility* (New York: W. W. Norton and Co., 1964), p. 136.

39. Julius Dresser, *The True History of Mental Science* (Boston: George H. Ellis, 1881), p. 30.

40. Quimby, *Manuscripts*, p. 62.

41. Ibid., p. 243.

42. Ibid., p. 173.

43. Ibid., p. 210.

44. Ibid., p. 227.

45. Ibid., p. 303.

46. Ibid., p. 231.

47. Ibid., p. 230.

48. Ibid., p. 231.

49. Ibid., p. 232.

50. Ibid., p. 327.

51. See Martin Marty, *The Righteous Empire* (New York: Dial Press, 1970), p. 114.

52. In his *Persuasion and Healing* (New York: Schocken, 1974), Jerome Frank discusses the common elements to be found in all American psychotherapies. In addition to the three cited here, Frank also argues that all successful therapies either explicitly or implicitly prescribe certain tasks or proceedings which help patients progressively master the goals envisioned in the therapeutic rationale. This fourth element is precisely what characterizes our many self-help psychologies and, as we will see, was a prominent feature of the New Thought movement initiated by Quimby's followers.

53. Quimby, *Manuscripts*, p. 191.

54. Frank, *Persuasion*, p. 27.

55. Quimby, *Manuscripts*, p. 319. Interestingly, Jerome Frank points out that the presence of religious elements in the healing process (such as Quimby implied) often facilitates cognitive reorganization: "The change in the convert's picture of himself in relation to the deity implies certain changes in his picture of himself and of others and changes in his patterns of social participation. The invocation of supernatural forces to support certain attitudes may resolve certain intrapersonal conflicts and so promote personality organization" (*Persuasion*, p. 81).

56. Cited in Dresser, *Health*, pp. 47–52.

57. Ibid.

Chapter 6

1. Mary Baker Eddy's indebtedness to Quimby has been the subject of heated debate. Julius Dresser's *The True History of Mental Science* (Boston: Alfred Budge and Sons, 1887) and his son Horatio's *The History of New Thought* (New York: Crowell Company, 1919) marshaled considerable evidence to show that Mrs. Eddy's writings were little more than garbled distortions of Quimby's unpublished manuscripts. Other detractors of Christian Science's foundress include Richard Dakin in his *Mrs. Eddy: The Biography of a Virginal Mind* (New York: C. Scribner's Sons, 1929) and Stefan Zweig in his *Mental Healers: Anton Mesmer, Mary Baker Eddy, and Sigmund Freud* (New York: F. Ungar Publishing Co., 1962). Mary Baker Eddy's most able apologists are Stephan Gottschalk in his *The Emergence of Christian Science in American Life* (Berkeley: University of California Press, 1973) and Robert Peel in his three-volume biography *Mary Baker Eddy: The Years of Discovery* (New York: Holt, Rinehart and Winston, 1966), *Mary Baker Eddy: The Years of Trial* (New York: Holt, Rinehart and Winston, 1971), and *Mary Baker Eddy: The Years of Authority* (New York: Holt, Rinehart and Winston, 1977).

2. Horatio Dresser, *History*.

3. Braden's *Spirits In Rebellion* is the most complete history of the Mind Cure or New Thought Movement. If we grant a certain affinity between Mind Cure and Christian Science, additional demographic information can be obtained from David Moberg's *The Church as a Social Institution* (Englewood Cliffs: Prentice Hall, 1960), Bryan Wilson's *Sects and Society* (Berkeley: University of California Press, 1961), and a doctoral dissertation at Washington University written by Joseph C. Johnson entitled "Christian Science: A Case Study of Religion as a Form of Adjustment Behavior."

4. Both Donald Meyer, in his excellent book *The Positive Thinkers* (New York: Doubleday and Co., 1965), and Gail Thain Parker, in her *The History of Mind Cure in New England* (Hanover: University Press of New England, 1973), offer extended interpretations of the feminist undercurrents of the movement.

5. Henry Goddard, "The Effect of Mind on Body as Evidenced

by Faith Cures," *American Journal of Psychology* (1896): 431–502.
6. Ibid., p. 498.
7. Ibid., p. 500.
8. Ibid., pp. 450, 453.
9. Ibid.
10. These stages were outlined in the first note for Chapter 5.
11. Examples of the mind curists' continued interest in mental healing and the mesmeric state of consciousness would be Anetta Dresser's *The Philosophy of P. P. Quimby* (Boston: Alfred Budge and Sons, 1895), Horatio Dresser's *Methods and Problems in Spiritual Healing* (New York: G. P. Putnam, 1899), Charles Fillmore's *Christian Healing* (Kansas City: Unity Press, 1909), and Warren Felt Evans's writings.
12. Representative New Thought texts would be Emile Cady's *Lessons in Truth* (Lee's Summit: Unity Press, 1894), Annie Payson Call's *Power through Repose* (Boston: Roberts Brothers, 1891), Horatio Dresser's *Living by the Spirit* (New York: G. P. Putnam, 1900), Charles Fillmore's *Twelve Powers of Man* (Kansas City: Unity Press, 1943), and the writings of Ralph Waldo Trine.
13. The self-help literature which tried to indoctrinate readers to make what Henry Wood called the "intelligent application of the laws and forces of the mind" to the practical conduct of life is exemplified in Charles Fillmore's *Prosperity* (Lee's Summit: Unity Press, 1907), Frank Haddock's *Power for Success through Cultivation of Vibrant Magnetism* (Auburndale: Power Book Library, 1910), Orison Swett Marden's *Peace, Power, and Plenty* (New York: Crowell, 1909), Elizabeth Towne's *Practical Methods for Self-Development* (Holyoke: E. Towne Co., 1904), and Henry Wood's *Ideal Suggestions through Mental Photography* (Boston: Lee and Shepard, 1893).
14. Both Horatio Dresser's and Charles Braden's histories detail Evans's contributions to the growth of the movement. The quotation cited here comes from John Teahan's "Warren Felt Evans and Mental Healing: Romantic Idealism and Practical Mysticism in Nineteenth-Century America" which appeared in *Church History* 48 (1979): 63–81.

15. Warren Felt Evans, *Mental Medicine: A Treatise on Medical Psychology* (Boston: H. H. Carter, 1873), p. 16.
16. Warren Felt Evans, *Esoteric Christianity and Mental Therapeutics* (Boston: H. H. Carter, 1886), p. 5.
17. Ibid., p. 46.
18. Evans, *Esoteric Christianity*, p. 149. Evans's second book, *Mental Medicine*, evidences this thoroughgoing reliance upon mesmerism in understanding his healing practice. His ideas about the mesmeric (impressible) state and the existence of animal magnetic fluids appear to have been greatly influenced by his reading of the German investigator Charles Von Reichenbach. Of additional interest is the fact that historian Charles Braden persisted in placing the word *hypnosis* in brackets wherever Evans used the terms *mesmerism* or *mesmeric state*. Braden's reconstruction of the movement is adversely affected by his own ideological biases, which exclude the very possibility of the unique spiritual state of consciousness attested to by the early mesmerists.
19. Evans, *Mental Medicine*, p. 266.
20. Evans, *Esoteric Christianity*, p. 153.
21. From one of Quimby's printed circulars as cited in Braden, *Spirits*, p. 62.
22. Evans, *Esoteric Christianity*, p. 1.
23. Evans, *Mental Medicine*, p. 53.
24. Evans, *The Primitive Mind Cure*, p. 87.
25. Mary Baker Eddy, *Science and Health* (Boston: Christian Science Publishing Co., 1875), p. 129.
26. Evans, *The Divine Law of Cure* (Boston: H. H. Carter, 1881), p. 42. Evans's Christian pantheism is in many respects similar to the category of panpsychism in contemporary process philosophy. Incidentally, most contemporary discussions concerning the rapprochement of religious and psychological conceptions of the self either implicitly or explicitly utilize very similar ontological understandings. See, for example, James Lapsley's *Salvation and Health* (Philadelphia: Westminster Press, 1972) or Gregory Baum's *Man Becoming* (New York: Herder and Herder, 1970).

27. Ahlstrom, *A Religious History*, p. 1019.

28. Evans, *Divine Law*, p. 266.

29. Evans, *Mental Medicine*, p. 104.

30. Horatio Dresser, *Methods and Problems*, p. 37.

31. Horatio Dresser, *The Power of Silence* (New York: G. P. Putnam's Sons), p. 116.

32. Ralph Waldo Trine, *In Tune with the Infinite* (New York: Crowell Co., 1897), p. 172.

33. Ibid., p. 16.

34. Ibid., from the preface.

35. Ibid.

36. Evans, *Esoteric Christianity*, p. 53.

37. Evans, "Learn to Contradict the Senses," *The Christian Metaphysician* 1 (1887): 5.

38. Cady, *Lessons in Truth*, p. 14.

39. Ibid., p. 62.

40. Once again, the New Thought can be viewed as the middlebrow formulation of the selfsame ideas then permeating the thinking of persons no less highbrow than William James. From his early essay "Reflex Action and Theism" to his later writings arguing for the philosophical supremacy of radical empiricism, James advocated the notion that our subconscious minds form the floodgates for the inflow of divine energies into human affairs. When Annie Payson Call wrote, "We learn how to allow the body to be perfectly passive so that it may react to the activity of the mind; and thus the mind itself should know how to be passive in order to react to the activity of the Divine Mind"—her words could not have more accurately conveyed the Jamesian spirit. We might remind ourselves that, in his public talks such as "The Energies of Men" and "The Gospel of Relaxation," James time and again lauded the writings of New Thought authors such as Annie Call, Horatio Dresser, Ralph Waldo Trine, and Prentice Mulford.

41. Evans, *Primitive Mind Cure*, p. 125.

42. Quoted in William James's *The Varieties of Religious Experience* (New York: Collier Books, 1971). Note that James was here illustrating his own theory concerning the metaphysical efficacy of prayer by quoting his former student, Horatio Dresser.

43. Wood, *Ideal Suggestions,* p. 41.
44. Wood, *The New Thought Simplified: How to Gain Harmony and Health* (Boston: Lothrop, Lee and Shepard Co., 1908), p. 135.
45. Wood, *Ideal Suggestions,* p. 12.
46. Ibid., p. 99.
47. Ibid., p. 97.
48. A lengthier discussion of the continuities between New Thought and the Protestant ethic can be found in both Gail Thain Parker's *History of Mind Cure* and Alfred Griswold's article "New Thought: A Cult of Success" in *The American Journal of Sociology* (November 1934): 309–318.
49. It is important in this connection to note Ralph Gabriel's account of the shift in Americans' understanding of personal prosperity in his *The Course of American Democratic Thought* (New York: The Ronald Press, 1956). "In the next decade, however, a significant change occurred in the success literature. The God of the Puritans faded gradually from the pages of the success books and was replaced by a strange and worldly mysticism called the New Thought. In the New Thought version of the success formula, the old virtues were still important, but new words and phrases appeared: 'personal magnetism'; 'mental control'; 'the subtle thought waves or thought vibrations, projected from the human mind' " (p. 165).
50. Meyer, *Positive Thinkers,* p. 121.
51. Parker, *History of Mind Cure.*
52. Horatio Dresser, *History,* p. 93.

Chapter 7

1. In actuality both of these owe a substantial debt to mesmerism for having generated popular support for new approaches to understanding, and healing, the human psyche. Historians of American psychology have totally ignored mesmerism, thereby giving the impression that the leap from Puritan moral theology to neurophysiological laboratories occurred in an intellectual and cultural vacuum. Henry Goddard's article which was cited in Chapter 6 would make an initial point of departure for pinpointing mesmerism's role in Americans' discovery of the "self." Another source should be Nathan Hale's chapter entitled "Mind

Cure and the Mystical Wave: Popular Preparation for Psycho-analysis 1904–1910" in his *Freud and the Americans* (New York: Oxford University Press, 1971). As for the part mesmerism played in stimulating both the psychology of religion and pastoral counseling movements, readers might give attention to the life and writings of the father of modern religious psychology, William James. In their *Pastoral Care in Historical Perspective,* William Clebsch and Charles Jaekle credit James with having inaugurated the modern phase of the cure of souls tradition. Clebsch and Jaekle deemed James's sympathetic treatment of the mind curists' theories worthy of inclusion in their collection of the classic documents comprising the Western heritage of religious care and guidance.

2. Ironically, neither side of the sacred/secular schism was able to embrace mesmerism's formulations about human nature. Adherents of both held mesmerist psychology to be untenable precisely to the degree that it approximated the other's methodological assumptions.

3. F. W. Meyers, "The Function of a Society for Psychical Research," *The Journal for the Society for Psychical Research* 1 (1900): 254–258. Meyers is an interesting candidate for the further study of non-normative religiosity in that he represents something of a bridge between high- and low-culture interest in the paranormal.

4. William James, *The Energies of Men* (New York: Moffat, Yard and Co., 1917).

5. James, *Varieties,* pp. 100, 102.

6. Quoted in Clebsch, *American Religious Thought,* p. 145.

7. William James, *A Pluralistic Universe* (New York: E. P. Dutton, 1971), p. 185.

8. James, *Varieties,* p. 259.

9. James, *Energies of Men,* p. 34.

10. The general affinity between James and the mind cure movement has been discussed at length by both Donald Meyer and Gail Thain Parker. Meyer notes that, "from Trine to Peale (Mrs. Eddy excepted, of course), William James counted as a chief authority for mind cure. His discussion of 'The Energies

of Men,' his reference to 'wider selves' of which men remained unaware, his fascination with the 'subconscious,' his overt and sympathetic interest in early mind cure itself, above all that general philosophy seeming to justify any philosophy 'that worked,' all qualified him as a hero in the loose pragmatism of the movement" (*Positive Thinkers*, p. 315).

Meyer argues that these apparent similarities pertain only to the surface of their respective philosophies. James, who had a deep appreciation for the "strenuous mood," espoused an ethical orientation to life that far surpassed the puerile self-indulgence which Meyers sees in the mind cure writings.

Parker takes Meyer's argument one step further and throws suspicion on the depth or integrity of the mind curists' interest in the subconscious mind: "None of the New Thoughters fully shared James's respect for spontaneous human powers. They craved reinvigoration, but sooner or later they wanted to harness new energies to the same old tasks. Before they had gone very far in paraphrasing James they turned to the topic of technique— how to get energy and how to use it. A cult of inspiration, whether based on Swedenborg or Bergson, was not for them" (*History of Mind Cure*, p. 159).

Neither of these commentaries—though unquestionably true in part—evidence awareness of the historiographical difficulties involved in comparing highbrow and middlebrow intellectual positions. Importantly, James did. He differentiated between the various "levels" of the mind cure paradigm and, in so doing, made important distinctions which somehow passed by both Meyer and Parker.

11. James, *Varieties*, p. 91.

12. Ibid., p. 102.

13. Ibid, p. 100.

14. James, *Pluralistic Universe*, p. 266 (italics mine).

15. James, *Varieties*, p. 100.

16. The particular use of the word *covenantal* here is based upon Richard Wentz's discussion of this theme of American religiousness in his *The Saga of the American Soul* (Landham: University Press of America, 1980), p. 80.

17. We demonstrated this point in connection with mesmerism on pp. 101–103.

18. It would appear that the mesmerists' healing practices almost perfectly exemplify Turner's description of the role of communitas in ritual healing. In this connection, we might note Turner's remark that religious healing is marked by the presence of powers which are felt "in rituals all over the world to be more than human powers, though they are invoked and channeled by the representation of the community" (*Ritual Process*, p. 106). He also observes that this power, or spontaneous communitas, " . . . is richly charged with affects, mainly pleasurable ones. . . . Spontaneous communitas has something 'magical' about it. Subjectively there is in it the feeling of endless power" (ibid., p. 139).

19. Henry Wood, *The New Thought Simplified* (Boston: Lee and Shepard, 1908), p. 10.

20. Turner, *Ritual Process*, p. 132.

21. Erik Erikson, *Insight and Responsibility* (New York: W. W. Norton and Co., 1964), p. 155.

22. Turner observes that as a paradigm of human possibilities, spontaneous communitas "cannot readily be applied to the organizational details of social existence. It is no substitute for lucid thought and sustained will" (*Ritual Process*, p. 139).

23. Don Browning, *The Moral Context of Pastoral Care*, pp. 103, 90.

24. Horatio Dresser, *Voices of Freedom* (New York: Knickerbocker Press, 1906), p. 172.

25. Ibid., p. 179.

26. Wood, *New Thought Simplified*, p. 135.

27. William James saw this clearly when he pointed out that the mind curists' healing practices did not justify their adherence to a monistic world view. James wasn't nit-picking when he insisted that their discovery of the healing power of religious receptivity could be more accurately accounted for within a pluralistic metaphysics: "I say this in spite of the monistic utterances of many mind-cure writers; for these utterances are really inconsistent with their attitude towards disease, and can easily be shown not to be logically involved in the experiences of union

with a higher Presence with which they connect themselves" (*Varieties*, p. 118).

James's point was that a person's metaphysical beliefs are the most significant things about his personality. Beliefs perform the all-important function of determining whether or not we inhabit a moral universe. As a psychologist, James could describe how beliefs transpose raw sensory data into salient images which call for certain types of response. As a moral philosopher, he championed those kinds of belief which elicit ethical conduct. And that was just the problem with the mind curists' belief in the illimitable power of our minds—it did nothing to establish the psychological foundations of moral self-understanding.

Selected Bibliography

PRIMARY SOURCES ON AMERICAN MESMERISM

A GENTLEMAN OF PHILADELPHIA. *The Philosophy of Animal Magnetism Together with the System of Manipulating Adopted to Produce Ecstasy and Somnambulism.* Philadelphia: Merrihew and Gunn, 1837.

A PRACTICAL MAGNETIZER. *Elements of Animal Magnetism or Pneumatology.* New York: Turner and Hughes, 1841.

A PRACTICAL MAGNETIZER. *The History and Philosophy of Animal Magnetism with Practical Instructions for the Exercise of This Power, Being a Complete Compend of All the Information Now Existing upon This Important Subject.* Boston: N.p., 1843.

BAYLEY, WILLIAM. "Some Facts in Mesmerism." *Proceedings of the American Society for Psychical Research* 1 (1907): 8–22.

BUCHANAN, JOSEPH R. *Buchanan's Journal of Man.* Cincinnati: Shepard and Morgan, 1849.

———. *Neurological System of Anthropology.* Cincinnati: N.p., 1854.

BUSH, GEORGE. *Mesmer and Swedenborg; or, the Relation of the Developments of Mesmerism to the Doctrines and Disclosures of Swedenborg.* New York: John Allen, 1847.

CALDWELL, CHARLES. *Facts in Mesmerism and Thoughts on its Causes and Uses.* Louisville: Prentice and Weissinger, 1842.

———. "The True Connexion of Phrenology and Religion." *American Phrenological Journal* 1 (1839): 1–24.

CARPENTER, WILLIAM. *Mesmerism and Spiritualism: Historically and Scientifically Considered.* New York: D. Appleton, 1889.

COLLYER, ROBERT. *Lights and Shadows of American Life.* Boston: Brainard and Co., 1838.

———. *The Manual of Phrenology.* Dayton: B. F. Ellis, 1838.

DELEUZE, J. P. F. *Practical Instructions in Animal Magnetism.* 2d ed., Translated by Thomas Hartshorn. New York: Samuel Wells, 1843.

DODS, JOHN BOVEE. *The Philosophy of Electrical Psychology.* New York: Fowler and Wells, 1850.

———. *The Philosophy of Mesmerism.* Boston: William Hall, 1843.

———. *Thirty Short Sermons, Both Doctrinal and Practical.* Boston: Whittemore, 1842.

DURANT, CHARLES. *Exposition, or a new theory of animal magnetism with a key to the mysteries: demonstrated by experiments with the most celebrated somnambulists in America; also, Strictures on "Col. Wm. L. Stone's letter to Doctor A. Brigham."* New York: Wiley and Putnam, 1837.

ESDAILE, JOHN. *Mesmerism in India.* Reprinted under the title *Hypnosis In Medicine and Surgery.* New York: Julian Press, 1957.

FISHBOUGH, WILLIAM. "The Macrocosm and Microcosm of the Universe Without and the Universe Within." *Library of Mesmerism and Psychology,* 1: 8–254.

FORBES, JOHN. *Mesmerism True—Mesmerism False.* London: Churchill Press, 1845.

GRIMES, JAMES STANLEY. *Etherology and the Phreno-philosophy of Mesmerism and Magic Eloquence: Including a New Philosophy of Sleep and of Consciousness.* Boston: James Monroe, 1850.

———. *The Mysteries of the Head and the Heart Explained.* Chicago: Sumner and Co., 1875.

HADDOCK, JOSEPH. "Psychology of the Science of the Soul Considered Physicologically and Philosophically." In *Library of Mesmerism and Psychology,* 2: 1–24.

JASTROW, JOSEPH. "On the Existence of a Magnetic Sense." *American Society for Psychical Research,* July 1886, pp. 116–27.

JOHNSON, CHARLES. *A Treatise on Animal Magnetism.* New York: Burgess and Stringer, 1844.

LÉGER, THEODORE. *Animal Magnetism, or Psychodunamy.* New York: D. Appleton, 1846.

Library of Mesmerism and Psychology. 2 vols. New York: Fowler and Wells, 1852.

MORLEY, CHARLES. *Elements of Animal Magnetism.* New York: Turner and Hughes, 1841.

POYEN, CHARLES. *Progress of Animal Magnetism in New England.* Boston: Weeks, Jordan, and Co., 1837.

————. *A Letter to Col. William Stone.* Boston: Weeks, Jordan and Co., 1837.

PUTNAM, ALLEN. *Mesmerism, Spiritualism, Witchcraft, and Miracle: A Brief Treatise Stating that Mesmerism Is a Key Which Will Unlock Many Miracles and Mysteries.* Boston: N.p., 1858.

REICHENBACH, CHARLES. *Physico-Physiological Researches on the Dynamics of Magnetism, Electricity, Heat, Light, Crystalization, and Chemism in Their Relations to the Vital Force.* New York: Clinton-Hall, 1851.

SANDBY, GEORGE. *Mesmerism and Its Opponents.* London: Longren, Brown, Green, 1844.

SARKAI, KESARI LAL. *Yoga and Mesmerism.* Calcutta: Elysium Press, 1902.

STONE, WILLIAM A. *Letter to Doctor A. Brigham on Animal Magnetism* (New York: George Dearborn and Co., 1837).

SUNDERLAND, LAROY. *"Confessions of a Magnetizer" Exposed.* Boston: Redding and Co., 1845.

————. *Pathetism:* Boston: White and Potter, 1847.

TOWNSHEND, CHAUNCY. *Facts in Mesmerism with Reasons for a Dispassionate Inquiry into It.* London: Baillerie Press, 1844.

SELECTED SECONDARY SOURCES ON MESMERISM

BURANELLI, VINCENT. *Franz Anton Mesmer: The Wizard from Vienna.* New York: McCann, Cowan, and Geoghegan, 1975.

DARNTON, ROBERT. *Mesmerism and the End of the Enlightenment in France.* New York: Schocken Books, 1970.

ELLENBERGER, HENRI. *The Discovery of the Unconscious.* New York: Basic Books, 1970.

GOLDSMITH, MARGARET. *Franz Anton Mesmer: The History of an Idea.* London: Barkert, 1934.

PODMORE, FRANK. *From Mesmer to Christian Science.* New York: University Books, 1963.

PRIMARY SOURCES REPRESENTING THE DEVELOPMENT OF
MESMERIST PSYCHOLOGY INTO THE NEW THOUGHT
PHILOSOPHY

*(Works Concerning Healing and the Mesmeric State of
Consciousness)*
DRESSER, ANETTA. *The Philosophy of P. P. Quimby.* Boston: Alfred Budge and Sons, 1895.
DRESSER, HORATIO W. *Methods and Problems in Spiritual Healing.* New York: G. P. Putnam, 1899.
DRESSER, JULIUS A. *The True History of Mental Science.* Boston: Alfred Budge and Sons, 1887.
EDDY, MARY BAKER. *Science and Health.* Boston: Christian Science Publishing Co., 1875.
EVANS, WARREN FELT. *The Divine Law of Cure.* Boston: H. H. Carter, 1881.
———. *Esoteric Christianity and Mental Therapeutics.* Boston: H. H. Carter, 1886.
———. *The Mental Cure: Illustrating the Influence of the Mind and the Body Both in Health and Disease and the Psychological Method of Treatment.* Boston: Colby and Rich, 1886.
———. *Mental Medicine: A Treatise on Medical Psychology.* Boston: H. H. Carter, 1873.
———. *The Primitive Mind Cure: The Nature and Power of Faith, or Elementary Lessons in Christian Philosophy and Transcendental Medicine.* Boston: H. H. Carter, 1885.
———. *Soul and Body: The Spiritual Science of Health and Disease.* Boston: Colby and Rich, 1876.
FILLMORE, CHARLES. *Christian Healing.* Kansas City: Unity Press, 1909.
QUIMBY, PHINEAS P. *The Quimby Manuscripts.* Edited by H. W. Dresser. New York: Thomas Crowell, 1921.
TROWARD, THOMAS. *The Edinburgh Lectures on Mental Sciences.* New York: Dodd and Mead, 1904.

Selected Bibliography

(Works Concerning Principles of Spiritual Regeneration and Personality Reorganization)

CADY, EMILE. *Lessons in Truth.* Lee's Summit: Unity Press, 1894.

CALL, ANNIE PAYSON. *Power through Response.* Boston: Roberts Brothers, 1891.

DRESSER, HORATIO W. *The Christ Ideal.* New York: G. P. Putnam, 1901.

———. *Health and the Inner Life: An Account of the Life and Teachings of P. P. Quimby.* New York: G. P. Putnam's Sons, 1906

———. *Living by the Spirit.* New York: G. P. Putnam, 1900.

———. *Voices of Freedom.* New York: Knickerbocker Press, 1906.

FILLMORE, CHARLES. *Atom-Smashing Power of the Mind.* Kansas City: Unity Press, 1949.

———. *Christ Enthroned in Man.* Kansas City: Unity Press, n.d.

———. *Metaphysical Bible Dictionary.* Kansas City: Unity Press, 1931.

———. *Mysteries of Genesis.* Kansas City: Unity Press, 1936.

———. *Twelve Powers of Man.* Kansas City: Unity Press, 1943.

TRINE, RALPH WALDO. *In Tune with the Infinite.* New York: Crowell Co., 1897.

———. *The Higher Powers of Mind and Spirit.* New York: Dodge Publishing Co., 1913.

———. *The Land of Living Men.* New York: Dodge Publishing Co., 1910.

———. *What All the World's A-Seeking.* Boston: Garr Co., 1896.

TROWARD, THOMAS. *Bible Mystery and Bible Meaning.* New York: Goodyear, 1913.

WOOD, HENRY. *God's Image in Man.* Boston: Lee and Shepard, 1892.

———. *The New Thought Simplified: How to Gain Harmony and Health.* Boston: Lee and Shepard, 1908.

(Works Making Intelligent Application of the Laws and Forces of the Mind to the Practical Conduct of Life)

FILLMORE, CHARLES. *Prosperity.* Lee's Summit: Unity Press, 1907.

HADDOCK, FRANK. *Power for Success through Cultivation of Vibrant Magnetism.* Auburndale: Power Book Library, 1910.

——. *The Power of Will: A Practical Companion Book for Unfoldment of Selfhood through Direct Personal Culture.* Auburndale: Power Book Library, 1907.

MARDEN, ORISON SWETT. *The Miracle of Right Thought.* New York: Crowell, 1910.

——. *Peace, Power, and Plenty.* New York: Crowell, 1909.

——. *Pushing to the Front.* New York: Crowell, 1894.

——. *Prosperity and How to Attain It.* New York: Success Magazine Inc., 1922.

TOWNE, ELIZABETH. *How to Use New Thought in Home Life.* Holyoke: E. Towne Co., 1915.

——. *Lessons in Living.* Holyoke: E. Towne Co., 1910.

——. *Practical Methods for Self-Development.* Holyoke: E. Towne Co., 1904.

——. *Making Money: How to Grow Success.* Holyoke: E. Towne Co., 1929.

WOOD, HENRY. *Ideal Suggestions through Mental Photography.* Boston: Lee and Shepard, 1893.

——. *The New Thought Simplified: How to Gain Harmony and Health,* Boston: Lothrop, Lee, and Shepard, 1908.

Index

Ahlstrom, Sydney E., 151, 196n.29
American nervousness, 112–14, 132, 169
anesthesiology, 12, 45, 187n.9
animal magnetism: as emanation of God's spirit, 86–88, 130; Mesmer's discovery of, 2; properties of, 4–5, 13–14; transference from healer to patient, 72, 124, 148, 192n.47, 203n.28; various terms for, 38, 39, 60, 70–71; as the vital force of the brain, 58
awakening(s), 74, 100–101, 117

Baird, Robert, 80–81, 83, 92
baquet, 6, 13
Beard, Charles, 112–14, 118
Bernheim, Hippolyte, 11
Bertrand, Alexandre, 11
Blavatsky, Helena P., 199n.72
Blithedale Romance, 35–36
Breuer, Josef, 57
Browning, Don S., 179, 185n.5
Browning, Elizabeth Barrett, 38
Buchanan, Charles: interest in neurological science, 65; on the practical applications of mesmerist psychology, 53, 67; on the relationship of science and religion, 54, 65–66; theory of mental impressibility, 53–54
Buranelli, Vincent, 186n.1

with an immanent divinity, 86–88; identification of the mesmeric state with the New Birth of evangelical religion, 86–89
Dresser, Anetta, 139
Dresser, Horatio W., 152–53, 162, 179, 190n.36
Dresser, Julius A., 139
Durant, Charles, 25

Eddy, Mary Baker, 30, 38, 88, 137–38, 150, 190n.36, 203n.27
Edwards, Jonathan, 84
electrical psychology, 60, 83, 86
Ellenberger, Henri, 186n.1, 187n.10
Elliotson, John, 11
Emerson, Ralph Waldo: as exponent of esthetic religion, 84; New Thought's reliance upon, 151; on mesmerism, 34; on Swedenborg, 92
Erikson, Erik, 126, 178
Esdaile, James, 11
esthetic religion, 83–85
Evans, Warren Felt, 139, 155, 157; advocacy of inner spirituality, 149–51; on Christian pantheism, 150–51; cured by Quimby, 146; early career as Protestant minister, 146; as healer, 147–49; role in transforming Quimby's healing practice into the philosophy of mind cure, 146, 190n.36; Swedenborgian influence on, 146, 151

Finney, Charles Grandison, 76, 77, 94
Fishbough, William, 83
Frank, Jerome, 133–34
Franklin, Benjamin, 7
French commissions' report on mesmerism, 7–8, 29
Freud, Sigmund, 12, 57, 126

Gassner, Johann Joseph, 3
Gladden, Washington, 111–12
God: identified with animal magnetism, 86–87, 129; related to man psychologically, 87–88, 128–30, 152
Goddard, Henry, 140–42

Goldsmith, Margaret, 186n.1
Grimes, J. Stanley, 56, 60, 69, 82, 92

Haddock, Frank, 160
Haddock, Joseph, 102
harmonial religion, 151, 196n.29
Harris, Thomas Lake, 95–96
Hartshorne, Thomas C., 29
Hawthorne, Nathaniel, 34–36
Houston, Sam, 70
hypnotism: contrasted with mesmeric state, 31; often (though incorrectly) used as a synonym for mesmerism, 12, 187n.9, 191n.39

industrialization's impact on the development of American psychology, 105, 109–11, 175

Jaekle, Charles, 185n.3
James, William, 169; as exponent of esthetic spirituality, 84; identification of the religious import of mind cure psychology, 170–72; recognition of mind cure's role in taking over the healing functions of religion, 169, 171–72
Janet, Pierre, 57
Jefferson, Thomas, 16–17
Jesus: as mesmeric healer, 199n.78; his nature defined in terms of mesmerist psychology, 129
Jung, Carl G., 12

Kluge, C. A. F., 192n.49

Lafayette, M. J., 16–17
Leger, Theodore, 83
Le Shan, Lawrence, 203n.28
Liebeault, Ambroise, 11
literary uses of mesmerism, 34–38

McLoughlin, William, 100–101, 102, 117
Marden, Orison Swett, 160
Mesmer, Franz Anton, 1–10, 13, 57, 59, 60; discovery of animal